Lessons From The Farm

a 31 Day Christian Devotional

by
David William Treat
with
Shirley Treat

Published by
Olivia Kimbrell Press™

Olivia Kimbrell Press ™

Rev. 5 : 13

David William Treat

Library Cataloging Data

Names: Treat, David William (David William Treat) 1947-

Title: Lessons from the Farm / David William Treat

Description: Olivia Kimbrell Press digital eBook edition | Olivia Kimbrell Press Trade paperback edition | Kentucky : Olivia Kimbrell Press, 2015.

Summary: True incidents in which God taught His principles through everyday life on the farm.

Identifiers: LCCN 2015955432 | ISBN-13:978-1-68190-030-8 (trade) | 978-1-68190-029-2 (POD) | 978-1-68190-028-5 (ebk.)

Subjects: LCSH: Devotions | Devotional daybook | Devotional works | Devotional literature | BISAC: REL012020 RELIGION / Christian Life / Devotional | REL012030 RELIGION / Christian Life / Family | REL012040 RELIGION / Christian Life / Inspirational | REL012120 RELIGION / Christian Life / Spiritual Growth | REL070000 RELIGION / Christianity / General | BIC: HRAB1 | HRCG9 | HRCL | HRCS | HRCV | HRCV9 | HRCX6 | HRLD | THEMA: QRAM | QRMP | QRVG | QRVS2 | QRVS3 | QRVX | QRVJ | QRVK

Classification: LCC Z688.C53 B72 2015 | 248.8'43—dc211

ENDORSEMENTS

I believe that Lessons From The Farm is the very best presentation of Godly stories that I have read. I commend it most heartily to all. I hope it will reach the ends of the earth for the great good I know it will do. I am very thankful for the abundant reference to Scripture for the better understanding of the truth, and the firmer faith which this book gave me.

–Rev. Donald B. Campbell
President of Jesus 4 U Ministries, Inc.

"A warm, heart-felt, and honest book that captures the essence of not only "farm life," but the very simplest tenets of daily life in a beautiful world. David William Treat captures you with each short story, simultaneously entertaining and teaching, and reminds each of us that God's love is simply limitless and profoundly apparent in all matters of life. Even if you live on a farm, don't live on a farm, or have never even been on a farm, this book is a must-read."

–Eric L. Long, M.D.

This is an engaging reading experience for those who understand the joy, and amusement, so commonly found in God's creation(s). It is wonderfully written, truthful and accurate. [Reminiscent of James Herriot's "All Creatures Great and Small"] in that it displays Dave Treat's unique ability to find humor, delight, fun, and, most significantly, the beautiful design of God's plan, through his own observations and his personal interactions with a few of God's creatures.

Believers and non-believers alike should be blessed through these carefully crafted lessons for life. Each story is told, just as they were experienced, through the eyes of one of God's true shepherds. I plan to have a copy on the coffee table at home and to gift a copy to the members of my Sunday School class. I wouldn't want anyone to miss this opportunity to measure their walk and current relationship with the Lord, while simultaneously experiencing such a sweet spiritual blessing.

–William W. Clough, Jr.

David William Treat

TABLE OF CONTENTS

ACKNOWLEDGEMENTS

God – May He receive all the glory and honor for the compilation of this book.

A special thanks to Marion Joiner. Without her "red pen editing" this book would have been left in need of serious grammar repair.

And to my wife and help meet Shirley – How could I ever finish this project without your encouragement, support, and labor in the office.

I love you, Dave

David William Treat

DAY 1: HENPHOBIA

For we know him that hath said, Vengeance belongeth unto me, I will recompense, saith the LORD. And again, The LORD shall judge his people. It is a fearful thing to fall into the hands of the living God.

Hebrews 10:30-31

I have coined a new word on the farm, henphobia. The medical term for fear of all chickens is Alektorophobia. I, however, only have a fear of one three-year-old black Dominicker hen I call "Getaway".

Not all hens are brooders, a term given to a hen that is willing to sit on a nest of eggs for 21 days and then raise the hatchling chicks until they can fend for themselves. This process entails scratching for food, finding the water dispenser in the chicken stall, and keeping them warm and safe. A good brooder is a great asset to any farm because she negates the need for an incubator.

Now Getaway was doing her job on top of the bales of hay, which were stacked in the barn. She had provided warmth and protection for eight hatchling eggs until they peeped out from their shells to experience conscious life for the first time. She had nestled herself and 14 eggs from different donor mothers, in between two bales of hay. The space was only large enough for her nest and a space against the barn wall.

We knew the chicks had arrived from the constant cheeps we heard as we entered the barn door. My wife immediately climbed up the bales of hay conveniently arranged in a staircase fashion. She was delighted to see the young chicks actively scooting about in the small space. Shirley was careful to go slowly as she approached the mama hen and her chicks. She verbalized softly to me on the barn floor that she saw at least six new chicks. I pondered the fact that God had put his seedtime and harvest principles even into chickens. I learned that even though fertile eggs are laid every day, until the hen starts to sit on the nest, the eggs are dormant. Her body heat and the constant turning of the eggs stimulates the embryos to life. Isn't God masterful?

As Shirley slid down the hay bales, she was voicing her concerns that the chicks were unprotected from predators, and where could they get water and food high in the top of the dry hay bales. It was then that I was privy to the safe "*plan*" for the new chicks and mama. The idea was for someone to climb up and catch the hen in a fishnet and transfer her to the chicken stall. Then *someone* would gather the darting young chicks, place them in a bucket and carry them to the brooder hen.

After a short discussion on who was better qualified for the impending *plan*, it was determined that I would be that someone.

As I climbed the notches of hay carrying the fishnet in hand, I noticed the hen was intently staring at me. Her head was peeking from behind the bale of hay. The top layer of hay only afforded enough room to crawl with one's head ducking the rafters of the overhead floor. I took the net in hand and as the hen flew upward from the crevice, I covered her with the net. She jumped higher, which only engulfed her more into the netting. "The *plan*" was working. I took hold of the side of the metal frame to seal her in, but in doing so, I exposed my wrist between my glove and jacket sleeve.

"Ow!" I yelled.

The same beak that could nurture baby chicks was able to inflict a bloodletting wound on my arm. First glitch in the *plan*. I managed to scoot to the edge of the hay and hand my wife the handle of the fishnet. She took the handle and pulled which allowed the big bird to fall to the bottom of the net. Away she went with bird in hand, headed to the chicken stall at the other end of the barn. In the meantime, I was sliding across the top of the hay to gather the peeping chicks. As I reached down into the opening I only saw four chicks. They had dispersed after mama left them.

I managed to catch them, and two others which had squeezed behind the second bale next to the wall. I then heard a peeping sound coming from the inside corner of the barn wall and saw a black chick which I snared with my empty hand. I called for my wife to hand me the bucket. Both hands were now gently trying to restrain seven tiny chicks before they could be placed in the "Mayflower moving tub".

I gingerly placed the future egg layers and early-morning crowers in the bucket. I heard yet another chirping behind my head, and I was now flat on my back trying to fulfill "*the plan*".

My hands now empty, I slid to the other side of the last bale of hay on the top row. Somehow a black chick had managed to find a tunnel in the hay and had fallen from the top bale trapping it against the wall. I grabbed the flashlight from my jacket pocket and, after peering over the first bale, I shone the light on the black chick. I reached down with my left hand pushing my face against the barn wall in order to afford me a longer reach. I closed my now gloveless hand and raised him to safety. With my flashlight in my right hand and the eighth chick in my left, I contorted like an inch worm across a leaf toward the edge of the precipice when I heard an "oh no" and I knew "*the plan*" had yet another flaw.

My wife yelled to me that the hen was out of the stall. As I raised my head, I heard the sound of a brooder hen full of wrath coming for a human who had unwittingly disturbed her perfect plan. I saw the hen as she crested the top of the bales through my outstretched feet. I saw her raise her wings, then pull them halfway back, assuming her attack mode. She started pecking at my feet while I was on my back.

I could only gently push her away, with my outstretched feet and at the same time screaming, "Get away, Get away", hence her name was born. She started pecking and jumping at me with her talons trying to get the peeping chick in my left hand. Still yelling "get away", my wife came with the fishnet and covered the raging "Heniac", taking her back to the chicken stall. Down from the hay, I placed the black chick in the room with its protector, my menace. All eight chicks back with mama safely cuddled under her body. Now, when I get too close to Getaway, she raises her wings and her voice at me, as if to say "come on make my day".

We need to be careful of "*the plan*" that we devise in ourselves. God judges his people, and He is capable of carrying a large rod of correction for His Beloved, and an even stouter rod of judgment for those that do not know Him. God may laugh at the plan that we labor over. Just give yourself over to Him, and He will carry out His perfect *plan* through your life.

QUESTIONS

1. What successful plan were you a part of at school, or at work, or at home that rewarded you with a sense of achievement?

2. Discuss the plan that went awry and the consequences that followed.

3. Have you ever felt His rod of correction?

4. Discuss the plan God has for your life as you understand it?

NOTES

DAY 2: BOBCAT

The thief cometh not, but for to steal, and to kill, and to destroy: I am come that they might have life, and that they might have it more abundantly.

John 10:10

I do not know why they called him Bobcat. If I was assigned the task of naming that critter it would go by the title of hellcat or Satancat. Bobcat sounds so unassuming, almost like a cartoon character. It certainly does not illicit the true character of the animal. All I can tell you is before he came to visit our farm, we had a total of 31 chickens. After he finished his rampage, we were left with three.

He would sneak in at different hours of the day or night, grab a chicken and run off back to his lair. No messy half devoured carcass was left like an opossum would leave, just one less chicken.

I was raised in the suburbs of Philadelphia, and the only Bobcat I ever saw was stuffed and on display at the Natural Museum of History. This one, however, was very much alive and prowling around the countryside seeking whatever he could devour. Although we never visually saw him, we did witness his destructive capabilities. Interestingly enough, the three surviving chickens removed themselves from the barnyard area and roosted in a tree near our house.

I would hope that you have seen the perfect parallel in this story to our own lives. We live this perilous life every day with our enemy, the devil, roaming about as a roaring lion seeking whom he may devour. (1 Peter 5:8). The verse also admonishes us to be sober and diligent. The three surviving chickens removed themselves from the dangerous area and sought refuge high up in the tree and close to their Master's house.

We too must remove ourselves from the dangerous areas where the devil can ensnare us in sin, and can then devour us. Isn't it amazing how we can lull ourselves into a sense of fake security and then the bottom drops out? We assume because nothing happened yesterday, that nothing will happen today. Jesus tells us not to be concerned for tomorrow for sufficient unto the day is the evil thereof. (Matthew 6:34)

Let us not be lulled into complacency, but rather keep our senses sharp, so we can recognize the schemes of our adversary. Recognizing the fact that he sends many kinds of temptations, sooner or later one of them will satisfy exactly what our flesh craves:

The chance for illegal gain to replenish our depleted bank account; a person who is a really good listener and only wants to "help" your marriage; a business deal you know in your heart is just not right. Whatever the device the devil uses to lure you, remember not to take a bite because he has placed a hook in there to pull you into deeper "hot water", and will eventually drown you.

Just as the Bobcat that I never saw, I knew he was real because of the destruction of my chickens. We know the devil is just as real and is continually plotting against us. If you want death, thieving, and destruction invite the Bobcat into your life. But, if you want life and life abundantly, ask the Lion of Judah to come and dwell within.

QUESTIONS

1. Can you describe another incident in nature that you witnessed with a similar outcome like the bobcat?

2. How can you better guard yourself from the destructive capabilities of your adversary the devil?

3. The chicken, which survived stayed close to the protection of the Farmer's house. Discuss ways you can avoid Satan.

NOTES

DAY 3: SEPARATION

For I am persuaded, that neither death, nor life, nor angels, nor principalities, nor powers, nor things present, nor things to come, Nor height, nor depth, nor any other creature, shall be able to separate us from the love of God, which is in Christ Jesus our Lord.

Romans 8:38-39

Ramalamb is a Katahdin ram weighing over 200 pounds. He has a sweet disposition, despite his size. He is a great combination, kind of like our God, bigger than our reasoning can comprehend, but with a love that spans the universe.

One Sunday morning before church, I went to the barn to feed as usual. When I entered the barn, I noticed one of the plastic barrels was overturned, with a couple of pounds of dog food strewn over the barn floor. I turned to check on the gate which keeps all the farm critters out, and my heart sunk when I saw that it was open. The last time this happened, two of the sheep had belly aches for three days. Later, I found two rabbit food sacks were chewed into, but all in all just minor damage this time. I had forgotten to latch the gate again.

I filled the pans with feed, and let all the sheep and goats into the barn except for Ramalamb. I had just put him on a diet, so I feed him separately outside of the corral. I put about three quarters of a cup of feed per animal in a 5 gallon bucket. After cleaning up the mess in the barn, I walked away and noticed the ram was pacing back and forth along the fence. I was busy picking up the remainder of last night's animal party when I heard a grunt and heavy breathing. I turned to see Ramalamb standing in the barn next to me. He had pushed down a 4 foot high hog wire fence wired to the shed entrance of the barn. The ram had never done anything like this before, so I started to analyze the situation. I checked his feed bowl outside, and found it to be full, and he was intently staring in the direction of one of the ewes. I swung the gate open and he quickly darted through it, right to the side of his waiting ewe.

Love cannot tolerate separation. It will find a way to overcome any obstacle that gets in the way, even a 4 foot high tensile steel wire fence.

Much the same as the Apostle Paul was writing about in the eighth chapter of Romans. What can separate us from the love of God, he muses, and then lists some things as tribulation, distress, persecution, famine, nakedness, or peril or sword. He then goes on to explain that we are more than conquerors through Him that loves us. Paul was persuaded that neither death, nor life, nor angels or principalities, nor powers, nor things present, nor things to come, nor height nor depth, nor any other creature, shall be able to separate us from the love of God which is in Christ Jesus our Lord.

Jesus endured the shame and pain of the cross so that we could share an eternity of joy with Him. Let's not let anything separate us from that perfect loving relationship we can have with Him.

QUESTIONS

1. Have you ever been separated from someone you love? Discuss how you felt.

2. Have you ever felt separated from God?

    a) Why?

    b) What did you do to bridge the gap?

3. Apostle Paul said nothing can separate us from the love of God, which is in Christ Jesus. In your own life experiences have you found that to be true?

NOTES

DAY 4: BAD DAY/GOOD DAY

My brethren, count it all joy when ye fall into divers temptations; Knowing this, that the trying of your faith worketh patience.

James 1:2-3

My day started just like any normal day on the farm. I put on my coat, gloves, hat and farm shoes that I keep in the laundry/mud room. As I was slipping my foot into my shoe, I happened to notice a sock protruding from the pant leg of my overalls. *So that's where the notorious sock monster hides his cache*, I thought.

I'm sure you have the same critter at your house. Think back to the time you put several pairs of socks in the washing machine along with your other clothes. When you retrieve them from the dryer you were one sock short – "SOCK MONSTER". Those missing single socks never show up again. This remains one of the great fun mysteries of life.

Proceeding out the door of the house, I looked in the direction of the gate which leads to the sheep pasture, and all the sheep had gathered at the gate knowing that I was coming to feed them. The four wheeler that we use to scoot around the farm was still in the backyard, and I had to open the gate, place a brick at the bottom to hold it open while driving through it. I chased the sheep back away from the opening, quickly got into the small vehicle and proceeded to drive through the gate. I was not fast enough, however, and Midnight our most mischievous ewe, bolted through the open opportunity to sample the dog kibbles in the bowls near the house.

Sheep are always willing to sample another type of food howbeit dog, chicken, rabbit, cattle or even human if it meets their nose test. She bolted through the open gate like a greyhound at the starting bell of a race, bringing several others with her. I gave up trying to stop the influx of sheep into the backyard. Immediately all the herd came into the open yard. *Oh well, good fertilizer,* I thought.

I drove the small vehicle through the opening into the pasture, leaving the gate open just in case the sheep wanted back in. Now, I raced to the pond to feed the ducks some corn. I'm always thrilled to see the four white ducks half running, half flying, to come and greet the chuck wagon. Picking up the gallon container I felt the emptiness of the container and remembered that I had not filled it the night before. Sadly for the "quackers," I headed toward the barn still hoping it was going to be a good day, at least from this point onward.

When I arrived at the animal barn I felt a slight drizzle of rain on my face, at least it's not raining I mused. As I opened the door, the scene inside was probably reminiscent of an explosion at a small grain elevator. Someone (me) had forgotten to latch the gate to the corral allowing the sheep access to the barrels of feed stored in the inner barn. After sweeping up the mess, I fed the chickens and rabbits without incident and my hope for a brighter day again seemed attainable. It was then that I heard the soft sputtering of rain on the metal roof of the barn.

That sound would be so enjoyable if I were listening to it from inside a warm bed, (somewhere between awake and first stirrings of consciousness.) But wait, I wasn't in my bed, I was headed outside to feed the cows. With two five gallon buckets in hand, I opened the door and stepped into the gentle rain. Not too bad I mused. I can get to the cattle feeder and back before I even get damp.

Unfortunately, the mechanical mule was in the repair shop so I had to use the four wheeler for the farm chores. It's kind of like eating peas with a knife, instead of a fork. A person can do it, but it surely is difficult. I balanced the buckets of feed on the back of the cushioned seat and drove gingerly to the cattle gate. The sheep were back in their pasture, and headed toward me. My loving wife had enticed them back with a little bit of dog food nuggets in a metal bowl.

"You are not getting any more to eat you brats," I yelled. I supposed they had enough to eat in the feed room at the barn. I reached the gate and stopped the ATV short of the chain, got down and unlatched the swinging gate. When I turned around the sheep were gathering about the vehicle. I jumped back, grabbed the handlebars and pressed the thumb throttle hoping I could get the ATV through the opening before the sheep had the opportunity.

Since thumb throttles are such a sensitive mechanism, I realized I had pushed it too hard and the small vehicle lurched forward capsizing the buckets of feed.

The sheep were quicker to respond than I was, and were already pushing and shoving each other to get the most they could for themselves. Watching the sheep, I recalled a similar scene at a church supper food line over dwindling desserts. I grabbed the buckets off the ground leaving most of the contents behind.

The sheep were in a frenzy, devouring the spilled feed, but I managed to scoop some of the cow food back into one of the buckets. I pushed the four wheeler through the gate, closed, and chained it. Climbing back on the seat and driving through the cattle to the feeding trough. Hmm, seems the rain is coming down much harder now as I saw water dripping from the bill of my ball cap. It was little trouble to dump the buckets in the feeders since they were only half full (not half empty as I consciously try to look on the positive side of things).

Returning to the gate I stopped to unchain it and climbed back on the seat. I pushed the thumb throttle and the engine died. I tried to start it again, but the engine just turned over and over, like it was not getting any fuel. (Did I mention that it was raining?) Then, looking down at the reserve valve used to turn on the emergency fuel supply, I realized the lever was already on reserve.

Therefore, it struck me that I was out of gas. I lowered my head onto my folded arms which were across the handlebars and rested my forehead. I didn't know whether to cry or laugh. The rain was falling from heaven somewhat faster now, and it was starting to trickle down the back of my exposed neck. With that cold sensation of rainwater, I made my decision. I sat up straight on the padded wet seat of the four wheeler, reared my head back into the face of the pummeling rain, and laughed. I mean a wholehearted belly laugh. Then a song came to mind:

"Did you ever have one of those days boys? Did you ever have one of those days? When nothing goes right. From morning to night. Did you ever have one of those days?"

The Holy Spirit brought to mind that out of the belly will flow rivers of living water. Also, that the joy of the Lord is our strength. I lifted my hands from the handlebars of the ATV and extended them to Heaven and praised God for the day that He had given me. Whether a good day or a bad day, they are all His days.

QUESTIONS

1. If you ever had a bad day, what made it so bad?

2. If you ever had a good day, what made it so good?

3. Knowing we will have another bad day, what could you do to make the bad day a little less bad?

4. Do you think your attitude can determine the outcome? Do you believe your attitude will direct your day one way or another?

NOTES

DAY 5: 20 & 12

He shall feed his flock like a shepherd:
he shall gather the lambs with his arm,
and carry them in his bosom,
and shall gently lead those that are with young.

Isaiah 40:11

It was New Year's Day in 2012. As we walked to the barn, my wife and I were filled with anticipation. My helpmeet and I had purchased two black lambs when we first moved to the farm and decided since they were black, to name them after ourselves. (Considering we were both black lambs in sin before the Lord washed us clean.)

One we called Shirley after my wife, and the other Davie after me. The next fall one of Davie's offspring named Midnight, was about to have her second litter. We entered the barn and rounded the corner of the stall where we had heard movement. Standing upright were two beautiful lambs, one black and white, the other pure white. My wife picked up the black and white which we immediately named 20. As I lifted the white one into my cradled arms we called him 12. Their names coming from the fact that they were both born New Year's Day of the year 2012.

With my right hand, I placed the lamb's body into my left arm. Quickly, the little white lamb nestled his head into the crook of my elbow, relaxing his body in my arms. As if I had done this a hundred times before, and completely trusting in the Shepherd that had gathered him up, my own heart began to melt. I realized this newborn fluffy and cuddly creature was so trusting to relax in the Shepherd's arms. The little Ram had been washed by his mother's loving tongue and was now clean and just about dry. Suspended four feet above the earth, he still felt no anxiety because he was secure in the protection of the one who cared for him.

The black and white lamb, however, in my wife's arms was antsy, wanting to be on firm ground next to his mother. The mother was gently grunting short calls to her young ones. She did not see either one of her lambs because my wife and I were holding them out of the scope of her vision. She was only looking down around the floor of the stall. After all, why would her little lambs be suspended in air. They should be walking on the dirt floor where they belong. The truth of the matter is that lambs do not look up. Unfortunately, Jesus referred to us as lambs. We do not look up often enough. We are reminded in the Scriptures to keep looking up, "for our redemption draweth nigh."

We as Christians, also have the free choice to either nestle into the Shepherd's loving arms or struggle to be released. Most people on planet earth are expecting us (Christians) to live like they do. Head down, eyes fixed on worldly things just like mama sheep had done. But we must remember that we are a peculiar people, our eyes are fixed on things above, because that is where our real Citizenship lies. The true Christian is accustomed to lofty things. It does not scare us when the Good Shepherd picks us up and sets us on higher ground. Rest in His arms church! He will not let us fall, nor lead us into wrong paths. Just keep looking up!

QUESTIONS

1. What one thing in your life keeps your head toward this earth instead of lifting it toward Heaven?

2. Does it make you nervous or peaceful to give yourself completely over to the Shepherd's arms?

3. What can you do to allow God more nurturing in your life?

NOTES

DAY 6: SLEEPY

It is vain for you to rise up early,
to sit up late,
to eat the bread of sorrows:
for so he giveth his beloved sleep.

Psalm 127:2

It was a beautiful spring morning. I was riding the four wheeler around the pasture checking on the perimeter fence. The cows were lying under the trees chewing on their morning feed, the squirrels were chattering on the tree limbs as blue jays were crying loudly. As I looked out on the pasture, one of my Dad's sayings came to mind: "God is in His heaven and all's right with the world".

The serenity and contentment I felt was only matched by the beauty of the surroundings that my eyes captured. As I was drinking all this in, my eyes gazed on a black lump on the hillcrest. It didn't look like a dog, although it was about that size, and besides we didn't have any black dogs. I drove toward the figure passing three or four large cows. As I got closer I realized the "blob" was a newborn calf. It was sprawled out on its side flat on the ground with its tongue hanging out of its mouth draped over the grass.

I dismounted the four wheeler and studiously approached the calf. Flies were all over his head. Shewing the flies away from the little bull's face, I feared the worst. I slid my hand under the side of his head, and lifted it up, no response. I thought I saw a shallow heaving of his chest, but there was still no movement in the limbs, and the eyes remained closed.

I lifted his head higher off the ground, hoping this would make it easier for the calf to breathe. Still no movement. I slid my hand under his head as far as I could, preparing to lift the calf to the barn before I called the vet. I was leaning closer in to my task, attempting to get a better hold on the animal.

At this point, his face was only inches from mine. We were eye to eye. As I was staring into this newly arrived face, his eyelids shot open, brushing his long lashes against my cheek. When his open eyes saw mine, he bellowed a loud maaah! He then proceeded to jump up on all four legs and began to run across the pasture at the speed of an Olympic track star. His tail was straight up in the air, his voice bellowing for his Mother, and he was running straight for the wire fence that separates our pasture from our neighbors.

I, on the other side of this sudden recovery had yelled just as loud as the calf. I was startled by a dying calf that had suddenly come back to life. As I was trying to rise to my feet, the unexpected explosive moment had propelled me backward. As I sat on the ground, I heard the Mama cow thundering past me in an effort to catch up to her newborn son. It was then that I started analyzing what had just happened and came to the simple conclusion that the little bull was just asleep. A deep sleep was afforded him, because he had no worries, no stress or anxieties, just, a full belly of Mama's milk and a contentment that he was going to be cared for. He was just plain tired from his new birth ordeal.

Should not we, who are the children of the Most High God, knowing that he cares for us, lay down our burdens and anxieties at His feet and just rest in Him. Remember the Scriptures admonishes us to be anxious for nothing. Sleep well tonight my Brothers and Sisters. God has everything in His control.

QUESTIONS

1. What is your typical reaction in an approaching thunderstorm?

   a) Climb into a bed and pull the covers over your head.

   b) Retract your head down into your shoulders and clench your fists.

   c) Go outside and get a firsthand view of the action in the sky.

2. Discuss what issues can keep you from falling asleep

3. Psalms 127:2 says that He giveth His beloved sleep. If we cannot fall asleep do you think we have a trust issue?

4. Do you think that sleep will be an activity we will do in Heaven?

DAY 7: LEAKAGE

And be not drunk with wine, wherein is excess; but be filled with the Spirit;

Ephesians 5:18

Here at the farm we have what we call the cement pond. It's not really a pond, nor is it cement. It is a vinyl lined in-ground swimming pool.

It measures about 55' x 25' with a diving board at the deep end. It has a step-out hanging ladder on one side and four steps with a handrail at the shallow end. The top has three horizontal rows of blue colored decorative squares made to resemble tile. When everything is working correctly, and all the chemicals are in balance, the bottom is vacuumed and free from leaves and dirt. When the decorative border is scrubbed, the whole pool sparkles in the sunlight.

However, there is a problem with the swimming pool: it leaks.

I have realized a parallel in the life of a Christian Believer and the leaking cement pond.

CHRISTIAN CHARACTERISTIC	POOL EQUIVALENT
Even when we filter out the things in our lives that is impure we still leak.	Filtering System
When we have removed the sin in our lives, we still leak.	Leaves and other debris
After we have worked on our character and integrity, we still leak.	Dirt & algae
Even after we have our bodies in good shape and we have eaten the right kinds of foods and nutrients needed, we still leak.	Pool chemicals
After we make ourselves outwardly presentable to God and to each other we still leak.	Tile rim around the pool
Just like the swimming pool, our spiritual containers leak.	Vinyl liner

Jesus referred to wineskins that have to be new to hold the new wine of our new nature. But even the best wineskins leak. Just as the pool's leak requires me to add back freshwater almost every day, we also must refill our spiritual wineskins with the water of the Word of God.

We may think that since it is only leaking a small amount, no one will ever notice that our water (Word) level is a little low. But we must remember that we, just as the pool, is being drained 24/7. Each and every day we are exposed to the world and its ways trying to dry up the purity and truth of God's Word in us. Even when we are asleep, our subconscious mind is taking us down avenues which are warring against God. We are in a constant battle to "bring into captivity every thought into the obedience of Christ."

Smith Wigglesworth, a godly 19th century Evangelist, kept his pool filled by reading the Word every 15 minutes. I realize with our busy and demanding lives, that four times an hour is impractical, but how about four times a day, or even one quiet time with God in His Word would help us be filled with His Spirit? As Brother Paul told us in Ephesians chapter 6, "the sword of the Spirit is the Word of God." Without that sword we are of no consequence in a harsh world full of battles.

Let's keep our wineskins (swimming pools) filled. They do leak you know.

QUESTIONS

1. Do you sometimes feel you are losing some of your memory?

a) As compared to 10 years ago?

b) As compared to 20 years ago?

c) As compared to 30 years ago?

d) Hey! How old are you anyway?

2. Considering we all want to be filled with God, discuss some ways to accomplish that.

3. Do you think you could come up with a patch to stop our spiritual leakage or do you think that God designed us that way in order to keep us coming back to the Fount of Himself to be refilled?

NOTES

DAY 8: KICKEN' & QUACKIN'

For I know the thoughts that I think toward you,
saith the LORD, thoughts of peace, and not of evil,
to give you an expected end.

Jeremiah 29:11

My wife decided we needed to have ducks on our pond. A woman who lives according to Proverbs 31, is a woman in which I take note. Not that she dictates her will in decisions regarding our farm, but God does speak to her heart and guides her. After all, we two are one in God's eyes. Then there is that practical wisdom in a marriage that says, "If mama ain't happy, ain't nobody happy".

We took a day trip to a hatchery in upper Tennessee. From the internet it made a great impression on us both. So we made a decision to go there based on beautiful photos of a picturesque farm nestled in between rolling hills with turkeys and chickens leisurely perusing the landscape for insects. When we got to the farm, we encountered a two mile, "pot holed" laden, dirt road leading to a small broken gate at the entrance to the driveway. The barn was not quite as easy to get to considering the mud holes and slippery inclines one had to traverse. Our poultry acquiring experience was not as beautiful as the website had pictured it.

Why is it we tend to make decisions based on what we see instead of what God tells us? By the way, we did not even consult Him in this endeavor. The Word tells us "to acknowledge Him in all our ways, and He will direct our paths". Proverbs 3:6.

The owner was nice enough to us, a slightly overworked, recently divorced woman who was trying to maintain a strenuous workload that had previously been shouldered by a married couple. Another unfortunate victory for the enemy's camp, I thought. Not only had a marriage been destroyed, but a viable working/business partnership as well. I was still looking for a partridge in the pear tree when we decided to finalize our purchase: four chicks, two bantam chickens, three polish chickens, and four buff Orphingtons.

When we arrived home, we transferred all the tiny feathered creatures to the homemade brooder box that I had constructed for their new temporary home. As the chicks grew in size, I was reminded how God takes care of us each day, and we should grow in the nurture and admonition of the Lord.

The day finally came when I had to remove the ducks from their plywood box home and release them to the vast expanse of the barn and barnyard. Once removed from the box the ducks huddled together quacking and scooting about the barn floor. Each day I came to the barn to feed and each time the ducks stood afar off until I had left the vicinity of the feed. They would not come near me even with the enticement of cracked corn. Even though I was faithful in feeding, watering and giving them shelter they did not trust me enough to get close to me. Considering the same set of circumstances, I ponder how similar man is to God.

The big day had finally arrived for the semi mature ducks, moving day. We needed to move them to our 150 foot round pond. I placed a mechanized mule next to the barn door with an open cage on the flat rear tilt bed. The ducks were inside the main part of the barn anticipating their daily ration of feed. We closed all the entrance doors in the barn, and I grabbed the trusty fishnet.

The ducks sensed something was afoot, and headed away from me and my net. My wife started to head them in my direction, and I gently swooped the net to the floor trapping one of the quacking ducks. (Side note – only female ducks quack loudly, males make more of a low hissing noise). My neighbor says you can always tell a female because she talks louder and more often than the males; he is referring to ducks I think.

One by one I loaded all the ducks into the cage kicking and quacking. With the last duck in the cage, I latched it and headed toward the pond. The ducks in the cage were extremely agitated at their brief captivity, and verbally let me know it. Upon arriving at the back of the pond, I placed the cage on the ground, door side facing the water. I unlatched the wire door and the "quackers" were pushing and flapping to exit their transport. As each duck was freed, they ran to the pond, into the water and immediately swam to the middle, the safest spot on the water. There was no hesitation on their part, it was as if they were born to be pond dwellers. Even though they were delivered to their new destiny by someone else's forcible hand, when they arrived, they realized this is where they belonged.

What a parallel to the Believer. We are gently moved to our new life in Christ by the Holy Spirit. We go most times not with hopeful anticipation, but rather much like the ducks, kickin' and quackin'. How much He loves us and tolerates our rebellious behavior, hoping once we get to the place He has designed for us, we will recognize that truth, and swim out into the still water He has prepared for us.

QUESTIONS

1. How have you seen God's hand of provision in your life?

2. Do you remember a specific time when you felt the leading of the Holy Spirit to move you in a specific direction?

a) Did you go in that direction and what was the outcome?

b) Was there a time when you rebelled against His nudging? What happened?

3. Do you think God wants us to utilize our potential for our lives or do you think He is concerned with His perfect agenda?

DAY 9: SILLY RABBIT

If the Son therefore shall make you free, ye shall be free indeed.

John 8:36

I built the cages for the rabbits plenty big enough so that each one of them could move around freely. They are California rabbits which sometimes grow to be quite large; some even weigh up to 15 pounds. I built three sets of cages, four across and hung them from the barn rafters so that the droppings would fall to the floor. I had not, however, counted on the prolificacy of these small mammals. We have all heard of the references to their reproductive capabilities. Trust me from personal experience, I can attest that they are all true.

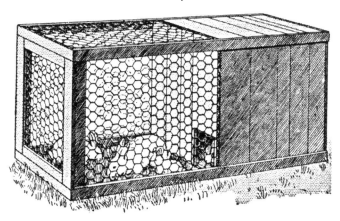

I constructed these cages with the rabbit's best interest in mind. They are high enough off the ground to keep predators from hurting the rabbits. They were large enough for them to move around freely making comfortable enough living quarters. There were water nozzles on each cage, and they are constantly supplying water from the large storage tank on the wall. They were fed every day with a good quality alfalfa pellet feed, and a little hay for them to nibble.

Obviously, everything a rabbit could want was wrapped up in these cages. The optimal word in this story is "cages". The dictionary defines cage as anything that confines or imprisons. (The rabbits had everything that they wanted, except for freedom).

One day as I was doing my daily chores feeding the rabbits, I latched one of the cages with a hook latch on the door, but I did not latch it tightly enough. I left the barn area after I had done my other chores and fed the rest of the animals.

That night, after coming out to the barn, I decided to check on the rabbits just to make sure that everything was all right. I looked up and down the row of cages and noticed one of the cage fronts was open. I walked up to it and noticed that the cage door had flopped down because the latch had not been properly clasped into the wire. I peered into the cage, fearing the worst but huddled in the corner, quietly and motionless, was the rabbit. Even though the cage door was open, the rabbit was so used to being caged that it never decided to escape.

Silly rabbit, I thought, you could have been hopping around the barn floor going anywhere you pleased, no longer hemmed up by the cage but rather free as the proverbial bird.

How often we as Christians do the same thing. We have been set free by the One who holds the keys. No longer are we in bondage to sin, or anything else that holds us back. We can worship with our whole heart not fearing any repercussions from anyone or anything that tells us to get back into the cage. The Scripture tells us, that, "He whom the son sets free is free indeed". We are free indeed. We no longer have to listen to the voice of the one who draws us astray. Sin no longer has a hold on us. True, it still lures us, but we have strength in Christ to resist. Sometimes we can be exactly like that silly rabbit that I just described, the cage door that once held us in bondage is wide open. Why do we not just walk in His freedom?

I was watching the movie "The Green Lantern" and there was one line in the movie when the star of the show was in training. His teacher said, "You are only limited to what you can do by the amount of will that you have." May I use that same analogy for Christians who are in training in Christ? You are only limited as to the things you can accomplish for God by the faith that you exhibit. That faith should be truly put into action when we are tested to see if our cage door is still open.

Before I came to Christ, I battled with depression. Sometimes my depression was so deep that I didn't think I'd ever climb out. By using my willpower, I was able to lift myself up but never out. The day I was born again, however, I was delivered from that demon, and have never had depression since. That familiar spirit comes back, however, with seven others worse than himself. He found that the door even though it's been opened, is not passable to him. I have been freed at last, and I never want to be imprisoned like that again.

Brothers and Sisters, let us not be like the silly rabbit, but let us be savvy Christians. For it is only when we recognize that the cage doors is open, we can escape. It's a far better life to live in freedom than in bondage to the evil one.

For those of you who are reading this, and don't understand what I'm talking about, you need to develop a relationship with Jesus Christ. Only through Him will you be totally free to live the life that Father God has planned for you. I beseech you by the mercies of God, allow yourself to develop that relationship, and fall in love with Jesus.

QUESTIONS

1. Are you comfortable and satisfied with the routine of your life? Why or why not?

2. Would you rather be satisfied or fulfilled?

3. Though Jesus has set you free, do you still have a draw back to the same sin which had you in bondage?

4. Knowing yourself, if you were that rabbit, would you have left the open cage or stayed in your comfort zone?

DAY 10: THE GARDEN OF EDEN TEMPTATION

And the LORD God commanded the man, saying,
Of every tree of the garden thou mayest freely eat:
But of the tree of the knowledge of good and evil,
thou shalt not eat of it: for in the day that thou eatest
thereof thou shalt surely die.

Genesis 2:16-17

When my wife and I were first married, we located a farm in Southern Indiana that needed a caretaker. I had just been laid off at a manufacturing plant in Indianapolis and we were in need of a place less expensive than what we were paying at that time. I talked with the owner of the farm, as he was a fellow employee of the company for which I had worked. We negotiated an agreement that was beneficial to both him and me.

The plan was that our family could move into the old (may I emphasize old) farmhouse rent free, with the stipulation my labor would also be given freely. I would be responsible to mend fences, feed the cattle in the winter, and bush hog the property in the summer.

My wife and I were excited to move into the farmhouse considering it was springtime and the daffodils and the peach trees were both bursting into new life. Just like a new "born again" convert bubbling with enthusiasm, we wanted to share this new life in Christ with anyone who would gladly listen and also with some who just tolerated the excited intrusion. It only took us a weekend in a pickup truck to move into our new two-story shelter. The owner lived in the city about 50 miles away, and he and his wife would only come down on the weekends to stay in a mobile home situated on the property.

There were 126 acres that made up the total landscape of trees, pasture, row crops and two ponds. The first pond was small, but deep. It contained lots of catfish which were excellent in sealing the lining of the pond because of their bottom feeding action. Bob, the owner, told us that we were welcome to fish and take as many catfish and snapping turtles as we cared to from the small pond. The other pond, which was about three to four acres in size, was picture-perfect. It had been built in a little valley between two rolling hills covered with mature deciduous trees.

The dense woods surrounding the pond, plus the sound barrier afforded by the rising landscape on each side, made it a very enticing place to visit. The pond had been stocked with bluegill and both small and large mouth bass. Considering it was a private pond, these fish were afforded the luxury of living without the threat of hooks in the water to shorten their lifespan. Sounds like a fisherman's paradise. I can just see the Apostle Peter relishing the thought of casting his net into this crystal-clear water. I, however, was not permitted to fish in this pristine watery paradise.

One day later that summer, I had done the things which were necessary. Just like the Apostle Peter, I went a fishin'. Yes, you guessed it, in the big pond. Although the smaller pond was fun, occasionally, I would catch a sunfish instead of a catfish. The lure of the big pond up on the high ground in the middle of the property proved too much of a temptation for me to resist. I got my fishing poles and some fat night crawler worms extracted from the garden, just to dangle in front of those, supposedly gigantic bass. I started my truck and excitedly drove to the small dam on the east side of the pond. My mind was imagining how Capt. Ahab was feeling as he set sail to capture Moby Dick, the white whale. I hiked around to a gently sloping bank on the south side of the water.

The birds were singing, the temperature was so comfortable, and my body was unaware if it was cold or hot. The trees were in full bloom and a breeze was gently moving the air like an old ceiling fan on low speed. I lifted my rod and cast my line into the water about 20 feet from the bank on the other side. I waited until my bobber stood upright like a soldier at attention, waiting for any disturbance below the waterline. I then took a seat on the green grassy bank.

I looked all around and saw that everything was pleasant to my eyes, except for the owner's small pickup truck, which had just crested the hill on the other side of the large pond. This was a Wednesday afternoon, he never came to the farm during the week only on weekends. I couldn't believe that the first time I had tried to sneak in a little fishing in paradise pond, I was found out. As he got out of his truck he looked at me in disbelief that I had done the one thing he forbade me to do. At that moment in time, I realized how Adam and Eve must have reacted when Father God came calling for them knowing what they had done, and how it grieved Him.

Every time I read or hear the account of creation, I understand that it truly is in the nature of mankind to rebel against the mandates of God even though they are designed with our benefit in mind. Let us all endeavor to strengthen our resolve to increase our resistance to temptation, so our relationship with Him is not hindered in any way.

QUESTIONS

1. Can you recall a time when you were doing something you knew you should not have been doing and got caught?

2. What prompted you to do that wrong thing?

3. Do you feel it is better to encourage someone to do right or is it more effective to dictate what they should not do?

4. Would you consider it a sin to be tempted?

5. Would you give in to the temptation?

NOTES

DAY 11: THE EMPTY BAG

Now the serpent was more subtil than any beast of the field which the LORD God had made. And he said unto the woman, Yea, hath God said, Ye shall not eat of every tree of the garden?

And the woman said unto the serpent, We may eat of the fruit of the trees of the garden:

But of the fruit of the tree which is in the midst of the garden, God hath said, Ye shall not eat of it, neither shall ye touch it, lest ye die.

And the serpent said unto the woman, Ye shall not surely die:

For God doth know that in the day ye eat thereof, then your eyes shall be opened, and ye shall be as gods, knowing good and evil.

Genesis 3:1-5

Andy is our only bottle-fed calf. He was born on a drizzly gray morning. I watched in heartfelt sympathy as the newborn calf's mother walked away from him. She dropped him as if he was a piece of unwanted litter left along the edge of the road. Just the same as a litter bug leaves his discard for someone else to pick up and place the trash in a receptacle where it belongs. The mama heifer was not interested in caring for the life cycle she had a part in creating.

I'm aware that there are several young people who can very easily relate to Andy's situation. Their own mother or father has divorced and they feel abandoned. Or the child who has just learned that he was adopted. And the two people who are raising him are not even his family. May I remind you that God has a special place in His heart for widows and orphans? James 1:27 Think of Jesus, who was raised from birth by a father who really was not his biological father at all.

I had just put the last of the feed from the 1000 pound feed bag into the five gallon buckets. I folded up the cumbersome bag the best I could and pushed it outside through the narrow door. I had designed it to keep the goats and sheep out of the barn's back room. I finally managed to get the entire crumpled four foot cubed bag completely out onto the concrete pad in front of the barn.

I then went back to finish feeding the rest of the

animals. As I exited the feed room, I was enthralled to witness the same inanimate feed bag I had thrown out earlier, had now become as animated as a Walt Disney character. Andy was now dancing, stationary on the ground, like popping corn inside a bag. The only aspect of this scene that was askew was the black rump and tail protruding from the open end of the bag. It was a humorous, enjoyable moment for me, but a very disappointing one for Andy.

This episode reminded me of how the devil promises lots of enticing things only to vanish with empty results. Such as the gambler who is down to his last $10 and is tempted to wager it in order to win the big jackpot. At his point of decision, does he give in to the temptation or stand strong and walk away.

Consider also the unwitting married man in the workplace who finds that he has become the target of a Jezebel who has set her sights on him. Should he succumb to her flattery and his carnal urge?

Completely forgetting that if he gives in, he will probably ruin his own marriage. An empty bag scenario for sure, becomes a point of decision.

Then, there is the student who has to pass the final exam with a high score in order to complete the course. Someone has mentioned that there is a paper with test answers for sale. One could pass the course easily with the purchased answers, but one could also be expelled if caught cheating. Point of decision: Should one climb into the empty bag, should one study and take the test with integrity?

The Word of God tells us that, "Sin lieth at the door, and unto thee shall be his desire, and thou shall rule over him". Sin is always at the door crouching ready to pounce on us whenever we stick our heads into that empty bag. Let us forever keep our focus on God, so we can rule over the sin that so easily can beset us.

QUESTIONS

1. What was one of the disappointments in your life?

2. Do you ever feel that if you had lowered your expectations that you would not have experienced a big disappointment?

3. II Corinthians 1:20 tells us that all the promises of God are yeah and amen in Christ. What guarantees do we have in the promises of Satan?

4. What promise have you made that you are a little lax in keeping?

NOTES

- -

- -

- -

- -

- -

DAY 12: DIRECTION BY INTIMIDATION

And whoso falleth not down and worshippeth, that he should be cast into the midst of a burning fiery furnace.

Daniel 3:11

On the farm there are goats and sheep. We have two kinds of goats, Fainting and Boer. The breed of the sheep is Katahdin. They are known as "hair sheep" because they do not have to be sheared for their wool; they are raised for meat. They have a tail which is about 16 inches long, and when the baby lambs suckle, they wag those little tails rapidly. (Very cute).

The goats and sheep, however, are stupid. I continually remind them to have patience when I am feeding because they quickly bump into me and each other. They race from pan to pan as I fill each one, and even push their way in between my legs as I am pouring out the feed. I have to remind myself that patience is a virtue and animals lack virtue. I can scurry fast enough to close the gate to the barnyard before they can come in from the pasture. The only method I have to use is my voice. Using a loud "Haahh" with my intimidator voice, they will turn and run in the opposite direction they were traveling. To get them moving where I want them to go, a loud shout and a wave of my hands prove enough of a threat to motivate them to follow.

The cattle cannot be led like sheep, but they can be

driven. If I stand and clap for the cattle and holler to them, they will only look at me stupidly but not come to me. But if I'm behind them and I start shouting and waving my hands, I'm able to make the move in the direction that I want. As always, I am behind the cow encouraging him to move in the direction I want. Placing obstacles in his path helps to guide him to the left or the right. They are much harder to intimidate however, as they are large and they know it.

How similar is that same method used by Satan and his followers when we are directed to move where he wants us to go. He will use peer pressure, enticement, embarrassment, threats, promises, finances, even the threat of death to turn us off of our straight and narrow path. In the book of James 1:14, Brother James reminds us however that "every man is tempted, when he is drawn away by his own lust, and enticed". We have to squelch our own lust and follow God's plan for our lives. If we do not, Satan will lead us in the direction that suits his plan, and we know he only comes not, but for to steal, and to kill, and to destroy.

So the next time that thief of the godly life comes yelling and waving his hands remember the following:

1. – Don't be intimidated, he has no power over you.

2. – Remind him that he was defeated by Jesus on that triumphal cross at Calvary.

3. – Rejoice in the victory as you stay your course that leads to life abundant and everlasting.

QUESTIONS

1. Have you ever been bullied by someone?

2. Which method are you more apt to respond to:

    a) Reasoning to come.

    b) Or pushing to go?

3. How do you get people in your charge to do what is needed to be done?

4. What method(s) do you think God uses to direct us?

NOTES

DAY 13: DRY CREEK

He that believeth on me, as the scripture hath said,
out of his belly shall flow rivers of living water.

John 7:38

How can it be a creek if it's dry I wondered? The back of
our property line is situated in the middle of a dry creek
that runs the whole length of our plot of ground. The
creek only runs when it rains, although in some places it
bubbles out of the rocky bed and flows for a distance
before it disappears underground again. When it does fill
up after a rainfall, it reaches a depth of 18 inches, and a
width of 14 feet. During a period of heavy rain, it gets even
deeper and moves quite rapidly.

Over the years the force of the water has caused
extensive erosion to the bank. The water has exposed
many tree roots, to the point where the tree could no
longer stand. There are several trees which have fallen,
usually across the creek, making it somewhat of an
interesting challenge to walk the creek bed in dry weather.
I have even had to run new fencing in some areas because
the old fence is dangling in midair.

The dirt that the roots were once firmly planted has
been completely washed away. Having exposed the
negatives about the dry creek, it is still one of my favorite
places to visit on a sultry day in August. Averaging 6 feet
below ground level, it has tapped in the coolness found
below the crust of the earth. To that add an adequate
amount of moisture from the wet rocky bed and
occasional pools of trapped water, resulting in God's first

original version of air conditioning.

Jesus told us out of our bellies will flow rivers of living water. The very core of our being is to be saturated with the word, the wisdom, and presence of God. We are to be springs gushing forth with life to all that we come in contact with.

Some of us (you know who you are) however, are too much like the dry creek. We have the capacity to carry a large amount of water, but are too often just a reservoir for small puddles.

Just as the rushing water in the creek exposed the root system of the trees at the bank, God wants to use His flowing river to expose the roots of issues in our own lives. Remember the fence that dangled in midair that our cattle were able to walk under that fence. To me it represented the boundaries we had set in our limitation to wading out into the river of life.

When the pressures and temptations of life get intense, we always seek out the cool place where we can be refreshed. I wonder what our life would be like if we sought out God and ask Him to fill our "dry creek" with His Presence. Perhaps we are trying not to allow the creek to get too full because it might completely immerse us in His life, and we would lose our own. But wait, isn't that what we are supposed to do?

Jesus said, "Except a corn of wheat fall into the ground and die, it abide alone: but if it die it bringeth forth much fruit". John 12:24 We need to be that corn of wheat. I have termed it "suicide by baptism". Paul said, "We are bound with Him by baptism unto death, even so we should walk in newness of life." We have to remember that we are dead to trespasses and sin. The old man has been washed away by the flood of the newness of life in Christ. We are no longer walking in the dry creek looking at small lifeless pools of shallow water. We are being carried along in a living water Jesus talked about with the Samaritan woman at the well. Come on everyone! Jump in, let's get wet together!

QUESTIONS

1. Have you ever been spiritually "dusty"?

2. What was that cause(s) of that deficiency?

3. Have you ever been saturated by the Presence of God? Can you describe how that experience felt?

4. What are some of the ways you can keep your spiritual creek from getting dry?

5. Have you ever built a spiritual dam that prevented others from receiving God's living water in their lives?

DAY 14: DECISIONS

Trust in the LORD with all thine heart;
and lean not unto thine own understanding.
In all thy ways acknowledge him,
and he shall direct thy paths.

Proverbs 3:5-6

We have had to make several decisions since we have moved to the farm. The first of which was what piece of property should we purchase. We looked at several which all met the criteria we had given to our realtor. Like a director searching for an actor, they all passed the screening, but none hit the mark. It was then our agent said. "I know the place that you would like; however, there's an offer on it already". He was right. We love the place.

God provided a way eight months later for us to purchase the farm. The original offer had collapsed, and the real estate broker remembered our name, called us. We concluded the whole sale via fax and two day airmail. Now that we had the farm, we had to decide what breed of animal we would raise. We looked into alpacas, no light at the end of the marketing tunnel. Beefalo was interesting, a much healthier animal than cattle to consume, but the public did not want to buy the end product. We finally settled on Black Angus cattle because that is what the consumer was desiring. But, more importantly, we prayed for God's wisdom to help us decide.

Shortly after starting to "piece meal" purchase our herd, my neighbor brought over two black Katahdin ewe lambs he was hoping to sell us. It was probably one of the easiest sales he ever made. We named the coal black lambs Davi and Shirley, to remind us that this was how we were before the Lord found us.

Next came the goats. We had four acres of briars and wild rose bushes that had claimed ownership. We decided on purchasing Boer goats because they were bigger, and we judged they could eat out the mess of weeds faster than a smaller animal, and also we consulted God.

Chickens, rabbits, dogs, cats, all were acquired much in the same manner. Did God speak a word into our ear on every selection? No. Sometimes He would have the right choice brought to us. I believe He even had doors that slam shut so that we would have to go elsewhere.

Don't worry about that decision you have to make. Just give it over to Him, ask for His wisdom, and He will give liberally the wisdom to those that ask. (James 1:5) God does not want us to struggle, He only wants us to rely on Him. If we do that, our faith is expressed in our reliance.

If you are having difficulty making big decisions, try building up your spiritual muscles by practicing on smaller ones. Proverbs tells us to trust in the Lord wholeheartedly, then acknowledge Him. The dictionary states trusting God means to admit to being real or true. Let's stop staring into our own limited bag of tricks and acknowledge the fact that God decided where to set the boundaries of the ocean. He is an expert at decision-making; listen to Him and He will direct your paths.

The most important decision that you will ever have to make in your life is the one that involves your eternal destiny. None of us will make it off this planet alive, that is a given. The choice we have to make is where we will spend our time after leaving here. The Bible clearly tells us in John 3: 16, "For God so loved the world that He gave His only begotten Son, that whosoever believes in Him should not perish but have everlasting life."

I would implore you to make that right decision before concerning yourself with any other decisions. After you decide to make Jesus your Lord and Savior all other resolutions will be guided by Him.

QUESTIONS

1. What was the best decision you ever made? What was the worst?

2. Did you consult with God before making the decisions referred to above?

3. Do you have difficulty in formulating a decision?

4. What do you think would help you make the next decision with wisdom and surety?

5. Have you made that one most important decision in your life, to accept Jesus as your Savior?

DAY 15: MIMIC

And God made the beast of the earth after his kind, and cattle after their kind, and every thing that creepeth upon the earth after his kind: and God saw that it was good.

Genesis 1:25

I believe that we should embrace the attributes of some of God's created animals such as those that follow:

The Cow: A true eating machine if there ever was one. The cow is perfectly built, so that her head reaches the ground in direct proportion to the length of her legs. She constantly moves her body along the grass in a pendulum motion, biting off small patches of the tender green shoots and swallowing them into her first of four stomachs.

When that stomach compartment has been adequately filled she will lie down on the ground and bring some of the contents of that stomach chamber into her mouth and start to "chew her cud". The process is known as rumination from the Latin word rumin which means "chew over again".

We as Christians should be as the cow in that we should be ingesting the bread of life which is the Word of God. After all Jesus said "Man does not live by bread alone, but by every word that proceeded out of the mouth of God. (Matthew 4:4) After we read the word (eat), then we need to bring it back to our remembrance later (ruminate) and meditate on it (chew the cud). Joshua told us to, "meditate on the Word day and night so that we can do all that is written therein". Remember the cow will starve if it does not eat, and so will you wither up if you don't feast on the Word of God. So we shall make our way prosperous and have good success.

The Bull: We have a handsome 1400 pound Black Angus bull on the farm. He is a muscular, mild mannered beast, who deservedly gets a lot of my respect. I named him "bull". As one studies Bull lumber through the pasture, it is impressive to watch his huge shoulder and rump muscles flexing in rhythm as he moves. No other bull in the herd is afforded the privilege of procreation with the heifers. He will strongly defend his superior position by "wrestling" with the smaller bulls in the herd.

This usually involves a forehead to forehead pushing match. Sometimes, the heads slip to the side causing the two male bovines to lock shoulders. Bull never shrinks away from any challenge, nor does he recant once he has accepted the challenge, and he always wins. After all, he has more mass and power than any of the other males.

The mature Christian needs not to back down from any battle with our adversary the devil. "Be strong and of good courage, fear not, nor be afraid of them, for the Lord thy God He is the one who goes with thee. He will not fail the, nor forsake thee." Deuteronomy 31:6.

We are to be strong in the Lord and in the power of

His might. Whatever the battle you are going through, don't back down. If you have been given a bad medical report, reread God's word that tells us how Jesus bore lashes on His back for our healing. If you are in financial trouble, first give an offering to a worthy cause with a cheerful heart. Then recall Psalm 1 that states: "That whatsoever you do shall prosper, for you are a righteous person in Christ".

Did you get accepted by the college of your choice? Then ask God which school He wants you to attend. Remember England's Sir Winston Churchill's mantra "never, never, never, never, never give up".

<u>Great Pyrenees Dog</u>: The Great Pyrenees breed of dog was first bred in the Pyrenees Mountains between France and Spain by Shepherds who wanted a large dog capable of guarding the flocks. The shepherds were harsh in their selection process, destroying the small, sickly or timid ones along the way. While protecting their charge, these massive woolly dogs have been known to fight to the death against insurmountable odds.

Our Great Pyrenees allows a child to lay on him, or a person to retrieve a bone he already has in his mouth. But he will ferociously chase after coyotes that come on our property. (Or the neighbors as well) These dogs don't just stand near you; they have to be leaning up against you. In fact, my dog actually places a big paw on top of my foot while resting his body on my leg. I guess he feels he can guard me better if I can't go anywhere.

Just a little side note here for you husbands. We are to love our wives as Christ loved the church and gave Himself for it. Protect your wife and respect the sanctity of marriage. Nurture and guard their spiritual walk as well as their physical lives.

And all of us need to guard our hearts. "Keep thy heart with all diligence, for out of it are the issues of life". Proverbs 4:23. When a sentry or guard is posted at an entryway, they are responsible for not only what comes in, but what goes out as well. Allow your heart to be filled with the good things of God, and then you won't have to worry when the overflow comes out. Jesus reminds us that "out of the abundance of the heart the mouth speaketh." Matthew 12:34b

<u>The Chicken</u>: Aah, the chicken, the purveyor of objects to fill a twelve slotted container. The edible egg that we enjoy at breakfast is only the end result of the story. Hens have an ovarian sac which accommodates multiple eggs, some tinier than a grain of sand. These tiny pellets wait to get a chance to come down the delivery shoot. The chicken is a perfect manufacturer of a product which is

transformed from a single cell to a fully developed egg.

We also have been designed by that same creative God who formed us in His image. Since He created the sun, moon, stars, and planets, animals, man etc., Should we not deduce He placed in us the same creative mind?

You are aware of a thought that suddenly has illuminated your conscious mind. You rattle it around in your brain like a pinball on the bumpers of its host machine. There seems to be validity in this "egg". I'm going to develop this and see what hatches. Remember, every invention, every exploration, every final act, began as a single thought. Be encouraged to let your good thoughts flow. Remember to dream big, and to think bigger, for we serve a big God.

The Squirrel: It is a fairly small critter if you remove its hair and bushy tail. But its lightweight size affords him the ability to climb trees and jump from the branch of one tree to the next tree. With this ability he constructs his nest high in the top of trees. Safe from most ground predators, it only has to be vigilant for hawks, owls or an occasional snake.

Like the ant mentioned in Proverbs 6:6-8, "Go to the ant, thou sluggard; consider her ways, and be wise: which having no guide, overseer, or ruler, provideth her meat in the summer and gathereth her food in the harvest. The squirrel gathers its food in the warm months and buries them in secret locations. So that if one or so of their caches are found by some other animal, it will still have plenty to last through the winter."

As followers of Christ, we need to build our "nests", a place where we live, as high and as close to God as we are able. We all know too well how the storms of life can cause the winds to shake us, but if we are rooted in Him, we will weather the storm. We need to store up some provisions and savings. Remember not to put all of your eggs (or acorns) in one basket. Diversify like the squirrel. It grieves me that a vast number of people in the church are debtors. Jesus wants us to be the head and not the tail. We are to prosper as our soul prospers. We should be able to give, to lend, to supply, and not just pay back our own debt. Down on the farm we use the expression "make hay while the sun shines". We are always to expect the storms of life, and to be ready to overcome.

QUESTIONS

1. If you had your choice to be any animal on earth, which one would it be and why?

2. Choose the best quality in five animals that you would like to integrate into your own life.

3. The Apostle Paul told his disciples to be followers of him even as I also am of Christ. I Corinthians 11:1, Do you find it easier to follow a Godly mentor rather than the written Word?

4. What does it mean to you to be a mimic of Christ?

NOTES

DAY 16: DANCER

And David danced before the LORD with all his might; and David was girded with a linen ephod. So David and all the house of Israel brought up the ark of the LORD with shouting, and with the sound of the trumpet.

2 Samuel 6:14-15

When I feed my cattle every day, they know that when I come out of the house they expect me to be heading to the barn in order to get their feed. As I walk toward the barn, all the cows line up along the fence, occasionally mooing, but all fixed on my every movement. The cattle are the last of the animals to be fed and they all impatiently wait by the fence much like fidgety marathon runners at the starting line of the final race.

The feeding troughs are several hundred feet past the gate into the pasture where the cows are waiting. I utilize my motorized mule to deliver the feed to the troughs. As the mule packing the ground feed on its small rear bed passes through the gate opening, she is waiting.

Bashan.

Standing clearly in my path looking directly at me with her head bowed almost in reverence to that which I am delivering. All of our animals are named with the exception of the chickens. We have named her Bashan, which from the Bible means fine pasture. Bashan is an area in the Middle East, where a fine herd of cattle is mentioned several times in the Scripture.

As the mechanized mule proceeded toward the feeder trough, Bashan is now walking backward. She has positioned herself about six feet in front of me. The full-grown heifer is now shaking her legs as she moves still backward almost doing a moonwalk dance. Her head swinging from side to side in rhythm to her front legs.

The cow knows what the machine is carrying and has at least a limited memory of how good it tastes. She does not take her eyes off of me. When I started making the right turn past the garden area, she made her move in the same direction. In total we traveled about 250 feet together, Bashan going backward and I forward. Her head swaying and bowing from side to side in rhythm to her legs.

This whole scenario would have been curious if it only happened once. But, this is an ongoing daily routine. All that I can relate is how excited Bashan was to receive what I was bringing. I must remember to allow myself an outward conveyance of joy that she displays. If animals could express emotions, shouldn't we?

We as people who have been delivered from darkness to light, bondage to freedom, sin to righteousness, eternal damnation to eternal life in God. When we come to church or anywhere we can be in His presence, should we not be excited to be with Him. Some of us are just eking out a mundane ritual of repetitiveness. Get excited Brothers and Sisters! He has set us free from sin and death. Keep your eyes on the eternal prize given to us by the Lord Jesus.

If you are willing to release yourself in Him, try changing some things. Maybe it will help to practice the following:

1. – Do you always sit in the same pew? Some of you have been in the same pew or chair for years. Changing your physical perspective may give you a different spiritual understanding.

2. – Attend a Bible study that teaches from the Word, not the opinions of man.

3. – Pray before you leave for church and get your heart prepared to worship before you open the door of the sanctuary. Listen to Christian praise music (not just pop hits) while you are getting ready to go to worship, and turn off your car radio. Then, when you arrive at church, your soul will be ready to focus on "The ark of God".

QUESTIONS

1. Some people don't dance for varied reasons, some do interpretive dance, and some others dance as David did with joy in their hearts for the Lord. Would you dance before the Lord? Why or why not?

2. How do you treat the Holy things of God? I.e. Communion, your Bible, worship etc.

3. Do you fully understand that the Word of God is truly the bread of life?

4. How can you improve on developing a more nutritious diet for your spirit?

DAY 17: QUACKERS

It is a good thing to give thanks unto the LORD,
and to sing praises unto thy name, O Most High:
To shew forth thy lovingkindness in the morning,
and thy faithfulness every night,

Psalm 92:1-2

"Hey neighbor, how are you all today? I just stopped to tell you that your ducks are in the road."

My neighbor down the way was always stopping by if he saw a problem on the farm, sometimes a cow would be out because of a broken board fence, sometimes a dog, sometimes sheep-this time it was ducks. I occasionally hired my neighbor as farm help, and I guess that's why he was so vested in what happens on the farm. I was very appreciative of the extra set of eyes that he used in watching over the farm. I'm not too proud to admit that I need help to run the whole farm. My neighbor can work circles around me, but is a little bit talkative. Then again, he is a salesperson.

We have Peking ducks, a breed that comes from China and is closely related to the Mallard duck. However, Peking ducks can't fly. I guess a direct result of interbreeding or overbreeding, I'm not a duck Guru, I just know I'm attached to these ducks. They are pure white in color from the top of their feet, to the beginning of their bill. Their feet and bills, however, are orange in color. They have non-descriptive black colored eyes, which constantly are alert and aware of their surroundings. They stare at me intently to see what I'm going to do next. You have probably even met a person like that, someone who stares intently at you, and you are acutely aware that there is nothing that you're going to get away with that they won't see. It may have been your boss at work, it may have been your preacher at church, and may even have been your weekend for Father. I have labeled it the Holy Spirit stare.

I normally feed the ducks twice a day, once in the morning and once just before dark. The other morning as I was driving out in the mechanical mule to feed the ducks, I noticed one of the ducks had blood all over her. The ducks aren't really tame, so it was difficult to really pinpoint where the blood was coming from. After several seconds I realized that part of her lower beak had been ripped off.

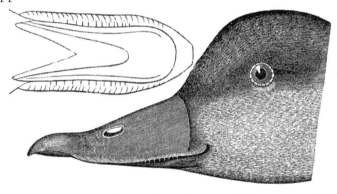

I was trying to determine what could have caused this terrible wound and finally came up with the answer of a snapping turtle in the pond. There was nothing I could really do for the duck; it was trying to eat the corn that was on the ground but having little success. So I put some corn in a little blue cup that we use to measure, and leaned down to her. She hesitantly looked at the cup lunged over and took a bite and backed off.

The second time she came back she started eating with

a frenzy and didn't stop until the cup was empty. Most of it had fallen out on the ground, but she did manage to get some of the kernels down her gullet. I reasoned that as long as she was eating, she would survive.

I have been working with the ducks since that time, and have found that inch by inch, little by little I can get closer to them. Now, I am even stroking her back and have one of my hands underneath of her belly. I would love to pick her up and really examine her for her wounds, but she seems to be doing very well so I'm going to leave well enough alone.

An interesting parallel is evident with these ducks and some Christians; they only come to me when they know that I have something to give them. They rush up the hill, wings flapping, quacking as they come, expecting to be fed and every day I try not to disappoint them. How often do we only come to God when we need something, when He has something for us, when we are just at our wits end and can't live without His provisions? That's the time that we come running to Him on our knees, on our faces with hearts longing to touch him, but only at those times does God see us running to him.

Wouldn't it be great to just set aside some time to tell God how much we love him? How much do we appreciate what he does for us, how much is needed in your life? Most times, however, we treat God as a candy dispenser. We just turn the knob of prayer and out plops a candy bar, or a pack of crackers, or even a sandwich or a drink.

Only when the duck was comfortable with me, and trusted me, would she come close enough to get what she really needed. She is now developing a closer relationship with me than she ever had before. As a matter of fact, I hate to admit this, but I probably give her a little bit more feed than I do the other three. Could it be that God is just waiting for us to trust Him more, to understand that He has everything that we need, in this life and the life to come? If a wounded Peking duck can trust her master well enough to get what she needs, we Christians can trust God for our every need.

You know the answer as well as I, but we have to press on, we need to go to Him when we need something true, but we also need to go to Him when we need nothing and just want to say "love you Lord". Can we not take a few minutes of our time each and every day to tell our Master; "thank you, and that we love Him".

President Abraham Lincoln, being the godly man that he was, never started the day without first talking to the Lord. He would place a chair across from his chair, and talk face-to-face with the Lord. You may find that you can address God directly from your bed, or on your knees, or in the still quiet place that you have set aside for that purpose. Whatever it takes, whatever you need to do, let's get quackin'.

QUESTIONS

1. When the Father's day comes, do you embrace it as an opportunity or does dread fill you and you try to avoid it?

2. Do you set aside a time of worship each day to show your gratitude to God?

3. When you run to God in time of trouble, do you also remember to thank Him?

4. What can you do to develop a more grateful attitude toward our heavenly Father?

NOTES

DAY 18: THE BLESSING

The LORD shall command the blessing upon thee in thy storehouses, and in all that thou settest thine hand unto; and he shall bless thee in the land which the LORD thy God giveth thee.

Deuteronomy 28:8

I met Donnie about two years ago. He was referred to me as someone who has hay for sale. I was definitely in the market for some large rolls of freshly cut grass. When I first met Donnie, it was evident to me that he was not a Christian.

Soon after our first encounter, Donnie's daughter was involved in a horrible automobile accident which claimed her life. My wife and I prayed for Donnie and his family. We sent a sympathy card with a hand written condolences and a prayer that God's grace would sustain him and all who knew his daughter through the process of grieving. Donnie started seeking answers. It just didn't seem fair that her life had been snuffed out in her teen years.

A horrendous life situation produces one of two responses when a calamity occurs in our lives. Either we are angry and blame God and turn away, or we run to Him for comfort and solace. Donnie wisely chose to run to God. While visiting with Father God, he decided to accept Jesus as his Lord and Savior. Donnie has not been the same since.

This year I telephoned Donnie to purchase new rolls of provender for this winter's feeding. He said he was already in the field that was closest to my house, and he would bring over three rolls on his already loaded trailer. What a blessing I thought, I will only have to unload his trailer with my tractor. But, I had only read the first page of what God was intending to do for me.

As he pulled his trailer through the gate, I was waiting with my tractor to unload the 1200 pounds, five feet in diameter, round bales of hay. As I started to transport the bales, I heard a grinding noise, and I just assumed it was a branch under the tractor I had picked up along the way. It was at that moment I noticed Donnie waving his arms in a criss-cross manner vying for my attention. I stopped the tractor and he pointed to the left front wheel. I climbed down from my seat and stared at a mass of mangled metal where the lug nuts used to be. The rim of the wheel was totally ruined to the point I would have to replace it with a new one. Great start to our hay gathering I thought.

We gingerly removed the three bales of hay from the trailer and set them on the ground. Hoping all the time the tire would not fall off the axle. I knew that we would be out of commission with the tractor for about 3 to 5 days. That's how long it usually takes to get parts from the dealer. I thanked Brother Donnie for his help and told him I would be in touch with him as soon as I got the tractor fixed.

The next morning as my wife was preparing to telephone the local part houses for a tractor rim, we got a call from Donnie. It seems he had been praying the night before asking God exactly who he could help this day. He told me that God had said that I was that person. He told me he had two tractors, a trailer, and a truck. If I would let him, he would be more than happy to bring the hay from the field to our pasture. I was overwhelmed with a sense of gratitude. First to Donnie, and then of course to God. Our omniscient Father God already knew the plight that I was going to experience. He had prepared Donnie's heart to supply my need.

About an hour later, Donnie pulled into the farm with his truck, trailer and his tractor on top of it. He drove the tractor off of the trailer onto our field. He then left with the empty trailer to go get three more rolls of hay. This process continued all day until we had 29 rolls of hay from the field.

After we had safely nestled the rolls in the garden area to protect them from the hungry mouths of the cows, Donnie reloaded his tractor onto his trailer. What a day it had been. One that was full of work, but full of joy at the same time. Rejoicing in the fact that my brother in the Lord would love me enough to spend his time and utilize his equipment to help me in time of trouble. As Donnie was preparing to leave our farm, I gave him a big hug and told him how happy I was that he had been obedient to God. He told me if I needed anything else to call and he would be right there.

I labeled what happened that day my blindsided blessing, (you could relate it to a pickup truck hitting you on the driver's side as your head was turned talking to your passenger. Only in a good way) I did not know that it was coming, but it overtook me just as the Scripture tells us, "God is always willing to bless His children". Think about it, when was the last time something just "fell into your lap"? It wasn't just a coincidence, it was a blessing from the Lord.

QUESTIONS

1. Give an example of how someone has blessed you in the past.

2. Blessings are not always measured in monetary gain. What are some of the other ways to determine a blessing?

3. What have you done in order to bless someone else?

4. Do you think that 'secret acts of Christian love' would be a good platform to launch a blessing?

DAY 19: PUPPY

Be not deceived: evil communications corrupt good manners.

I Corinthians 15:33

Puppy is a sweet hoot of a dog. He is a third-generation of litters stemming from a Great Pyrenees female given to us from some people living in Nashville, Tennessee.

Her previous masters told us that she was difficult to keep at home. That proved to be an understatement. She got impregnated by our neighbor's border collie. Fortunately, we were able to find homes for six of her seven puppies. But Bernie, her seventh puppy, was destined to become a part of "It's a Treat Farm".

Her mother "Snowy" was a gentle heart, and that personality trait was passed on to Bernie. She reminded me of a St. Bernard when she was young, hence the name Bernie. She grew up to be a beautiful dog with blonde and white long fur resembling a medium-size collie. Her good looks, however, proved to be too much of a temptation for a wandering pit-bull, and she conceived presenting us with seven pups nine weeks later, déjà vu.

We were able to place six of those puppies in someone else's home, but the last puppy, well, that's how "Puppy" came into our lives. This 'left behind' offspring has proven to be a sweet tempered dog with quite a few antics to make us laugh. Sometimes after returning from the barn he is waiting for me. With the speed of the slow-motion shootout victim, Puppy falls on his back to the ground, his legs swinging straight up into the air. He stays in that position, because in his memory banks he knows that I will scratch his belly, and I usually prove him right.

Puppy is not unlike us; he has a susceptible nature that is drawn to the dark side. He seems to do better when other influences are not around. By that I mean our neighbor's dog, which is a sweet Labrador retriever when he's in the front yard, but when he's in the pasture, he becomes another dog. He starts chasing the cows, but soon switches to what he especially enjoys, chasing the little calves because they are more his size. He runs them until they are exhausted, and I'm always afraid that they are going to put a foot into a hole and break a leg, or worse. The Labrador runs straight at the calf; meanwhile, Puppy comes around the outside edge and traps the animal in between the two dogs.

The first time I saw this maneuver, I couldn't believe my eyes. The fact that Puppy would join in such debauchery willingly, is an unpleasant thought for my brain to digest. The poor calf was caught in the middle, and only when the mama cow came to his rescue, the dogs ran the other way. It was like both dogs had teamed up to do evil, because that is what each one expected of the other.

I have seen several good people go down the same pathway. They are in church making good headway toward the new creation of Christ in them. They are tithing, volunteering for everything, and worshiping with their whole heart. Then one Sunday they don't show up for service. When I truthfully tell them that they were missed, they give me excuses such as, "I had to work" (Boss influence), "I had family coming and I had to prepare dinner (Family influence), "I just couldn't get out of bed" (Party friends influence). I even heard of the story of a fellow that renamed his boat so that when his wife was asked where he was, she could truthfully answer he was out on "Visitation".

If we try long and hard enough, we can justify just about anything. If we can't find something to justify our decisions, we can always ask someone else. There are lots of folks outside of the church body that would be glad to give many reasons to go down the wrong path.

We always feel that we can be a positive influence in

someone else's life. But Apostle Paul tells us that method doesn't work because the darkness always attempts to overshadow the light. Just as Puppy was drawn away by the neighbor's dog, we too can be drawn away from the 'straight and narrow path' that Jesus instructed us to travel. I believe that is why He told his disciples to go out in 'twos' because one would strengthen the other. Let us all stay the course, and watch out for 'the neighbor's dog'.

QUESTIONS

1. Do you think man is inherently good or evil?

2. Have you ever been enticed by someone to do wrong?

3. While you were committing this wrongful act, did you consider what God thought about it?

4. After the act had been committed, did you worry about what God thought?

5. How can we as professing Christians keep on the straight and narrow?

DAY 20: LIGHTS OUT

Finally, brethren, whatsoever things are true, whatsoever things are honest, whatsoever things are just, whatsoever things are pure, whatsoever things are lovely, whatsoever things are of good report; if there be any virtue, and if there be any praise, think on these things.

Philippians 4:8

My wife and I also run a bed and breakfast at the farm. We both have been in the "people business", Shirley, was the CEO of a Staffing Corporation and me, as a Pastor.

We tried to make the surroundings at the farm as comfortable and as festive as we can. There are tiny Christmas light bulbs on a string and we have the seating area of the pool deck decorated by six strands of these lights. When I first hung these tiny lights, I was pleased at the warm glow of the illumination it gave to the surroundings of the swimming pool area.

The next night, however, when I plugged in the strands, my eyes immediately went to the light bulbs which were not working. It seemed I was more adept picking out what was wrong, rather than enjoying all the bulbs that are glowing properly.

Apostle Paul tells us we should think on the positive things in life. Things which are true, honest or honorable, just, pure, lovely, of good report, of any virtue, and if there be any praise think on these things. How often do we concern ourselves with the negative things of life, such as gossip, how we will fail, distrust in other people, catching a cold, flu or worse?

I am also reminded that Jesus told us that we also are the "light of the world;" tiny Christ-like bulbs reflecting the light of God to a dark and dying world. I imagine Jesus is also concerned if one of our lights goes out, but for a different reason. He is concerned about the candle (us) that is illuminating this world, as well as the absence of light. We need to keep our wicks trimmed, and our lights held high.

The world is looking for any and all opportunities to point out that another light has burned out. Unlike the manufactured bulbs, however, we can get our light burning again just by going to the source of the light. He is able, willing, and desires to restore us to our fullest capacity to give off that precious light to a dark and dying world. Just ask him to reignite your life's light.

QUESTIONS

1. Do you view a glass containing 50% liquid half full or half empty?

2. Considering that Jesus refers to the church as His bride, do you try to find faults or imperfections in an earthly bride? What do you see?

3. How should we as Christians respond to that light that is out? Ignore it, replace it, repair it or criticize it?

4. What can you do personally to acknowledge the lights that are on rather than those that are out?

NOTES

DAY 21: WATER THE BEANS

And God said, Let the earth bring forth grass, the herb yielding seed, and the fruit tree yielding fruit after his kind, whose seed is in itself, upon the earth: and it was so.

Genesis 1:11

A few days ago I mailed my youngest grandchildren some dried pinto beans and some instructions. They are being home schooled, and I thought that this would make a good learning project for them.

I emphasized they should choose a quart size or bigger clear glass jar. Take some paper towels and line the inside up against the glass. Place the beans about half way down the container in between the towel and the glass, so that the seed is trapped against the glass. When all the beans are in place, slowly pour some water into the glass so that the paper towel is saturated and there is about one inch of water in the glass jar. Then place the jar carefully on a windowsill of a very sunny window.

Our daughter then explained to the children that God had created the most perfect perpetual design ever. Seedtime and harvest are brilliantly designed so that seeds that are planted grow into plants that eventually mature and produce more seeds, some to eat and some to plant and make more of that same seedling. In the case of their experiment, it will produce more pinto bean plants.

In the directions I explained that it was imperative that they never let the jar run out of water. The water is the life giving force that softens the shell of the seed so that the roots and stems can break through the shell. It also stimulates the seed to grow roots going down and stems rising toward the light.

The seed will continue to grow as long as the moisture is supplied to it until it uses up all the nutrients in its own seedpod. At that point the tender shoot has to be planted in prepared, good soil so that it can continue to grow with the proper amount of sunlight, nutrients from the soil, and water the bean plants moisture into mature seed-providing plants.

This story is about the water, or maybe the seed, perhaps the root. In actuality it is about the Son. Without the water the little sprout could not break out of its hard shell. Neither could the roots absorb the needed life-giving nutrition. I can't help but reflect on John 4:14b – "…but the water that I (Jesus) shall give him shall be a well of living water springing up into everlasting life." Jesus is the only supplier of the water we need for our "bean" to prosper.

In Matthew 13, Jesus explained the parable about the sower. A sower is one who plants a seed. He said that some seed were devoured by the enemy. Some were sown on ground that was too shallow, and the roots could not grow. Some were sprinkled among the thorns which are the cares of this world and the deceitfulness of riches which chokes out the little seed. But the seed that was planted in good, prepared soil allowed the seed ample source to put its roots down, thus allowing it to grow.

I understand Jesus was equating the seed to the Word of God, but we are also seeds that have been planted in a dark world. We need to keep our soil fertile. We can enrich our soil by cultivating it with the Word and good preaching and teaching. We need to intertwine our roots with other like-minded Christians to hold each other upright, just like the giant redwood trees do in California. Then we need to bask in the Light. Jesus said, "He was the light of the world and those that follow Him shall have the light of life." John 8:12.

Before we plant our garden, we always till the hard soil first. The action breaks the rigidity of the soil while uprooting any weeds and grass before planting our seeds. The human heart in the natural or under regenerated state is full of evil. From the heart comes forth lying, cheating, adultery, even murder. The heart of man is his soul per se. It is naturally filled with hard soil. But when we are "born again" by the Spirit of God, it starts to become rich and enlightened to be able to receive the seed of the Word of

God. We must maintain the seed of our heart in order that the seed planted by God will develop into a fruit producing place used mightily by the Spirit. Jesus said, "We will know them by their fruits."

Let's allow the good seeds of God to be placed in our fertile hearts and let them grow in the light of the Son, and don't forget to water "the beans".

QUESTIONS

1. Have you ever forgotten to water your potted plant or garden? Describe what happened to your plants.

2. If we assume we are seeds that God has planted in a dark world, do you feel like you are growing?

3. Do you consider it your responsibility to water someone else's seed?

4. Do you have any objections to letting God prune you in order for you to produce more fruit?

DAY 22: BROWN EGGS

Judge not, that ye be not judged. For with what judgment ye judge, ye shall be judged: and with what measure ye mete, it shall be measured to you again.

Matthew 7:1-2

I was boiling some of the eggs collected from my chicken coop. My ladies (that's what I call our chickens), are great layers and always produce more eggs than I need. The eggs from this particular breed of chickens, is the color of milk chocolate. Looking into the boiling water, I remembered some of our other chickens, how they had given us dark chocolate, white shelled, and even blue-green colored shells.

They were all eggs, about the same shape and size even though some were small pullets from my first time layers, and some were extra-large from a mature hen. All were eggs, all from chickens; all had been fed the same feed. They were all producing a protein-rich source of food, but were all presenting different colors of shell.

After the eggs began to boil, I covered the pot, turned off the stove, and left the eggs to solidify for 15 minutes. When the time had elapsed, I emptied the boiling water into the sink and let a small stream of cool water trickle over the broken shells to loosen them.

As I started peeling back the cracked shells, I was awed by the contrast of chocolate brown next to the bright white of the solidified previously clearer albumen. It was the same white I had seen when I had peeled all the other colors of eggs. As I studied the purity of the now naked egg, I was reminded of the Sunday school song;

Red and yellow, black and white

They are precious in His sight

Jesus loves the little children of the world.

The Bible tells us that man looks on the outside appearance, but God examines the heart of man. I used to determine someone's worth by their clothing, or the residence where they lived, or even the job that they held. God reminded me that everyone's soul is equally important in value.

Jesus said, "Judge not, lest ye be judged." Surely we have all seen people who are so quick to point out flaws or wrong doings of others. Somehow they believe this will make them look better than the other person and make them feel better about themselves. But we, as children of God are to attain to the image of Christ, not just a little better than our fellow believers.

Even when my egg shells crack when I boil them, I still use all the eggs to make my egg salad. God is not concerned about the color of our shells, our overall size, or even if we have some cracks (flaws). After all, the Scripture tells us that there is none righteous, no not one.

There are many reasons that we should be going to church, or Bible studies, or *Koinonia*. Koinonia is defined as a transliterated Greek word which means communion, joint participation; the share which one has in anything, a gift jointly contributed, a collection, etc. It identifies the idealized state of fellowship and unity that should exist within the Christian church, the body of Christ.

We can build up one another in the Faith, edify each other, not gossip about the faults of another. Remember, we are all in this boiling pot of water together. I believe if we examine ourselves closely we might even see a few cracks in our own shells.

QUESTIONS

1. An honest soul-searching question would be: Are you prejudiced against any one person? It could be because of his or her race, sex, I.Q., the area in which he or she lives, or religious denomination.

2. Do you feel there are second class citizens, church members, or occupations?

3. Do you think that every man, woman or child was created in the image of God?

4. What can we do to reveal the similarity of all 'eggs'?

NOTES

DAY 23: PERSONALITY

[For my determined purpose is] that I may know Him [that I may progressively become more deeply and intimately acquainted with Him, perceiving and recognizing and understanding the wonders of His Person more strongly and more clearly], and that I may in that same way come to know the power outflowing from His resurrection [which it exerts over believers], and that I may so share His sufferings as to be continually transformed [in spirit into His likeness even] to His death, [in the hope]

Philippians 3:10 – Amplified Version (AMP)

On the farm, as in our town, as in any city, as in the whole world there are personalities. The dictionary defines personality as, "The sum total of the physical, mental, emotional and social characteristics of an individual."

Let's examine our largest ewe sheep "Midnight". She is large and black, mother of many, she is strong-willed, and a true leader, even over our 250 pound ram.

No matter how hard I try, I can't seem to get her to change her ways. I have disciplined her with the rod of correction. I have lured her with sweet feed, (which does work while she is eating), given her voice commands, physically chasing her, even giving her "the look" does not seem to change her mischievous ways. If I have the door to the barn or a gate open, even a smidgen she noses her way through it. If I direct her to an open gate that I want her to enter, she goes the opposite way.

Then there is "Carmel" a blonde-colored sheep who will not even come close to a human, even though she was born on our farm like most of the rest of the herd.

Another example is our 1200 pound Black Angus bull (whom I have named "Bull", pretty creative huh?) is large enough to charge me and my motorized mule and do some serious damage. He has never tested for weakness in our fences, but rather chooses to lumber along passing through any gate I open in front of him. He even enjoys a vigorous scratch on his head.

We have two cats, a Siamese (named Si Si) who could care less if I petted him or even spoke to him. As long as I feed him, he tolerates being a part of the farm family.

We also have a tabby cat (Kitty Kitty) who was caught in a live trap in the barn, and released. I reckon she is grateful for the release, because she has never left. She jumps on my shoulder when I come close enough to the partial walls that separate the stalls, and loves to ride on the toolbox of the mechanical mule when I make my rounds.

These are just some of the personalities I have noted on the farm. These individualities I have mentioned, though, belong to another genus. What about Homo sapiens? We have all the qualities that animals possess, but in addition have a soul. The truly alien part of us is so very important to the God who created us and all living creatures. The animals I previously described do not possess the ability to change their basic makeup, we do.

We are all born into sin (Psalm 51:5). But the good news is just because we start out in sin, as sinners, there is a way out. His name is Jesus.

Those of us who know Him have come to the realization that we have the opportunity to become new creatures, or a new creation because of His work on the cross. If you know Him, then you can experience that His new nature has been born again in you.

The animals react upon instinct because that is all that is within them. We can also respond to our natural instincts, but we have to change them from a carnal mind to a spiritual mind. I recall the wristbands and other accessories which read WWJD (What would Jesus do?).

It was a great tool to get our mind focused on Jesus, but as we mature in Christ, shouldn't we put on the mind of Christ, and make His nature our own? Remember, after we are born again in Christ, we have a new different nature, a new mindset, a new outlook, and a new personality.

QUESTIONS

1. Of the four basic personality types, which one best describes you?

Sanguine – Enthusiastic and an extrovert.

Phlegmatic – Calm, not easily rattled.

Melancholy – Soberly thoughtful, pensive.

Chloric – No nonsense, leadership ability.

2. Do you find other personalities enjoyable or offensive?

3. Describe the personality of Jesus.

4. Are you in the process of allowing God to 'tweak' your personality?

DAY 24: VERY SATISFIED

I have been young, and now am old;
yet have I not seen the righteous forsaken,
nor his seed begging bread.

Psalm 37: 25

Birds, squirrels, rabbits, serpents, cattle, sheep, goats, as a matter of fact, all of the animals that God has created do not have to be righteous in order for Him to supply their needs, and to watch over them. I have never seen a bird sitting on the edge of a used tuna fish can beg for some seed. I have, however, witnessed birds at their feeder loudly chirping through the window for me to fill their empty container.

I realize that we have all seen starving animals, but most times these are a result of failures of mankind to take his rightful place of dominion and shepherding over God's creation. Since the very beginning of creation, God has put into place for this world to continue to function in perfect seed time and harvest and reap production as He had engineered.

All of my farm animals know that they only have to look to me in order to be fed. They don't have to struggle by going long distances to find food. The grasses are available to them in the pasture in the summer, and rolled bales of hay in the winter. Even the wild birds that live around our farm, know to check the bird feeders, and look for any scraps that might have been thrown on the ground.

At the farm we are almost overrun with squirrels. We call them tree rats because they are so plentiful, as well as a nuisance. They are constantly at the dog bowls sneaking kibbles of food from the bowls, and running off with their stolen property. Our apple trees were doing well this year growing to a good size; however, the squirrels got all of them first and took them off the tree. We never get anything because the squirrels can easily maneuver up high and take them before we can even think about harvesting them.

The point is the animals understand where to get their food. We have to tend the garden. From Genesis 3:19, "In the sweat of thy face shall thou eat bread, till thou return unto the ground, for out of it wast thou taken: for dust thou art, and unto dust shall thou return." Nevertheless, our Father is still Jehovah Jireh, our provider.

I have a saying which embodies the whole message of the story. "Don't sweat the small stuff." We need to not entertain the "what if" or "suppose this or that were to happen". We cannot allow the uncertainty of this world to creep into our faith life. From Philippians 4:19, "But my God shall supply all your need according to His riches in glory by Christ Jesus." All of the animals on our farm, even the wild birds in fact, understand that God will take care of them. They don't stress, they don't fret, and they just rely on Him. If the animals "get it" don't you think we should as well?

QUESTIONS

1. At this point in your life are you one of the following:

    a) Discontented

    b) Usually fulfilled

    c) Very satisfied

2. The Apostle Paul said, he was content in whatever state he found himself in. How could he say that considering all the trials he went through?

3 Did you ever think there was a point in your life where God would not take care of you?

4. The scripture I Peter 5:7 says, "Cast all our cares upon Him because He cares for us." Have you managed to do that?

NOTES

DAY 25: WATER

In the beginning God created the heaven and the earth. And the earth was without form, and void; and darkness was upon the face of the deep. And the Spirit of God moved upon the face of the waters.

Genesis 1:1-2

In the beginning God created our planet, which contains earth and water. They were not created separately, but rather together making up our third rock from the sun.

The earth's surface is made up of about 71% water, the human body contains about 60% water, two parts hydrogen to one part oxygen. Both elements in their natural state are gaseous elements, but get God involved, put them together and it becomes a life sustaining liquid.

While serving as a Hospital Corpsman in Vietnam I had the unfortunate experience of surviving three days without water in tropical conditions. An unforgettable hardship that I never want to repeat. Now when I feel the first pangs of thirst, I stop whatever I'm doing to extinguish that old memory of body-craving thirst.

At the farm the chicken waters are constantly running out of water. I never knew chickens could drink so much. The rabbits are watered by a gravity flow system from a 30 gallon plastic barrel, but the hoses are constantly popping off and draining the main tank. The cattle are supplied water by a 40 gallon neoprene tank with an automatic float system. The tank is always full using this system unless the supply line is inadvertently shut off. If that tank goes dry, the cows are the first to let me know by their bellowing. Even our flowers, shrubs and trees exude a warning sign when they get dehydrated by their wilting leaves and flowers.

Wouldn't it be wonderful if we had an alarm system built into our spirit to warn us of impending dangers? A lot of us go along day by day enjoying the sunshine and the good days, and we tend to slack off in our spiritual watering until we meet someone who has just been in the presence of God and is drenched by the washing of water by His Word. Or perhaps we get into a real "jam" such as a sickness or sin and now realize we were not walking as close to Him as we thought.

The best way to stay full of the liquid of spiritual life is to be a fruit inspector, not everyone else's, but our own.

Are your fruits supple and good tasting? Or are they bitter, tasteless or even caustic?

Have we helped our neighbor who was in need, encouraged the one that was down, given of ourselves even when it was inconvenient. The apostle Paul encouraged young Timothy to stir up the gift that was in him. We are ultimately the ones who are responsible for our own water pots. So I would encourage each of us to weed our garden of life, water our seeds by the Word of God, and give our lives plenty of Sonlight to grow to maturity.

QUESTIONS

1. Have you ever seen a goldfish jump out of its bowl? Describe the regression steps that happened to the fish if he is not returned to its bowl.

2. How would you describe your own spiritual water meter?

    a) Void of moisture like an almond.

    b) Shriveled up like a raisin.

    c) Supple like a ripe banana.

    d) Saturated like an orange.

3. If we get into the condition of spiritual dryness how can we re-hydrate?

NOTES

DAY 26: THE BALCONY
By Shirley Treat

He that dwelleth in the secret place
of the most High
shall abide under the shadow of the Almighty.

Psalm 91:1

One of the highlights of living here on the farm is slipping away to the upstairs balcony off of the Rhode Island Red room. It is only a 6 x 10 space, but the time we share together there is priceless. I become isolated from the news, work, and problems of life. Some days, the problems are too many to handle. So we sit, sip coffee, and leave everything behind.

My husband Dave and I look out over the farm that takes more time and money than we ever thought we would have to invest. To see this 24 acre rolling hill farm we have been blessed to have and care for is still unbelievable.

The farm also takes care of us. We see all the animals waiting for our daily special time with each of them. Deer are often in the bottom area that brings an excitement each time they pass by.

To think this is a new day in Christ and what all will He bring today. He gives us peace that passes all understanding. To sit in awe of the love and blessing and more gifts than we could number or think of. To be a child of a King and baste in His presence to know everything is going to be all right. No matter what! To look over at the

Godly man He has given me to walk through this life and at times to share the heavy loads.

We are never alone. Yes, this hiding place, balcony, or the great escape. It is special to me to enjoy my best friend, coffee, laughter, decision making, and time with my Lord. We relax, take a few deep breaths and enjoy this wonderful time together.

Who said we can't have it all? God said, 'I'll give you the desires of your heart"! Come on... sit a spell. He is waiting for you in your special place.

QUESTIONS

1. Where is your favorite place to go to get away from it all?

2. Where is the place you go to get closer to God?

3. The Psalmist tells us that "He is the restorer of our souls." What does that mean to you in your own life?

4. Give three steps you would take to allow God to flood your soul.

NOTES

DAY 27: MY NEIGHBOR

Neither go into thy brother's house in the day of thy calamity: for better is a neighbour that is near than a brother far off.

Proverbs 27:10b

The poet Robert Frost once said that good fences make good neighbors. It turns out just the opposite has been true in our case. Our next-door neighbors have been one of the highlights of moving to Southern Tennessee from Florida.

Our newfound neighbors and now friends have been a Godsend to my wife and me, as newly arrived outsiders. The people in rural Tennessee are extremely nice, but hard to fit in with since everyone knows everyone. But who are you?

I love the colloquialisms that the people express, such as "we're proud to have you", "Just ain't "no count no more". Our neighbors have been farming all their lives, so they had a vast knowledge of life on the farm. I once confessed that I believe he has forgotten more about farming than I ever knew. Every time I have a problem with the animals that I can't figure out, I call him and within minutes he is at the gate in his pickup truck honking for me to open it.

Our little fainting goat was trying to deliver a kid that was really too large for her and she was having a terrible time, screaming at the top of her lungs in pain. We were sure that neither mother nor kid would make it through the ordeal. Eurice recognized the fact that the kid was much too large for the birth canal. The father had been a large boer goat, and not really suited for breeding with such a small nanny goat such as this black-and-white that we called Oreo. We did lose the baby goat, but managed to save Oreo thanks to our neighbor.

Eurice's wife Jo is always sharing a pot of beans or a special dessert with us. She sings in the choir at the large Baptist Church outside of town. I really enjoy and love her, even if she is a Baptist (just pokin' fun). I truly believe without the support, knowledge, sharing and encouragement of these two neighbors, our time of settling in would have been shaky. Even if my own Brother had been closer, he probably could not have helped us more than our next-door neighbors.

Maybe you have been planted by God in a place where you could be a good neighbor and lightening the load of someone you live close to. We have a hand painted plaque on our kitchen window and it reads: "Friends are God's way of taking care of us". Try reaching out to someone on your street or neighborhood; you might be surprised to find your neighbor's problem could be remedied by you.

By the way, I was not born or raised on a farm, but I believe Philippians 4:13 where Paul says, "I can do all things through Christ which strengthens me". Especially when I have a close neighbor that helps in times of trouble.

QUESTIONS

1. How close do you live to your blood relatives?

2. Do you have a good enough relationship with them to ask for help in time of trouble?

3. Do you have a good enough rapport with your neighbor to call upon them in time of need?

4. An even more important question is could or would your neighbor illicit your help in their time of need?

NOTES

DAY 28: BROCCOLI

And Jesus answered him, saying, It is written, That man shall not live by bread alone, but by every word of God.

Luke 4:4

It was a very enjoyable meal, but too much food. The steak was juicy with just the right amount of spices. The baked potato caved in under the weight of the knife that was cutting it. The ranch dressing was of the homemade variety.

I learned a long time ago that ranch dressing not only spreads better over potato, but tastes creamier than sour cream. The warm, dark whole-wheat just from the oven rolls were sweet from the baked in honey. With or without butter they warmed your taste buds.

Then there was the broccoli.

Bright green in color because it had been steamed, not boiled into a lifeless, colorless, limp mass. It stood firm on the plate, but tender enough that it could be easily chewed. Ah yes, I thought, another fabulous meal at the Junkyard Dog restaurant. The leftover food was scraped into a Styrofoam container, and we carried it home. Usually, we get so busy talking after dinner, we forget to take the leftover food with us, but not this time.

When we arrived home, I took the Styrofoam box of food out to the pasture to feed my big dog Nanook. He was excited to see me, but ecstatic to smell the steak scraps. I gave him the steak first, piece by piece so he wouldn't choke himself gobbling down the good stuff. I placed the open container under his chomping jaws. He always smacked them together at the anticipation of food. He dove into the baked potato slipping the skin into the back of his massive jaws and the potato with the ranch dressing disappeared under the overlapping jowls.

Next was a small piece of broccoli. Nanook placed the whole of the piece squarely in the middle of his mouth, then he froze. He was perfectly still all over, much like a bird dog when he senses a quarry in a bush. He was processing this new food in his brain. Deciding that he didn't like the taste, he promptly opened his mouth and the whole un-chewed piece was spat out to the ground. He then picked up the pieces of whole-wheat roll and walked away with it in his mouth. The only thing left was the difficult to degrade Styrofoam container and one piece of broccoli.

God gives us blessings all the time, some are easy to digest, money, a better job, a beautiful child, divine health.

Yet, the Lord also gives us trials, testings, demands our obedience, and our sacrifice. How often do we spit out the things that would make us better Christians just because they don't feel right in our lives.

We reject temptations because they hurt, instead of counting them all joy which will increase our faith if endured. We choose not to fast because we feel we are just too hungry, forgetting the fact that denial will produce spiritual ears that are more receptive to hear God's voice.

Just as broccoli is a wonderful food given by God to keep the body healthy, some of the more unpalatable things in life improve our relationship with Him. As to the Styrofoam takeout, which carried the food to Nanook last a very long time in a landfill. The Bible carries the Word of life to us, and it last for all eternity. Enjoy… your broccoli!

QUESTIONS

1. Have you ever eaten a particular food that you just found unpalatable? What was it?

2. The Bible is known as the bread of life. What is your most favorite verse to ingest?

3. Has the Word of God ever spoken something to you that you found to be bitter?

4. Do you think that a maturing Christian should accept the Bible as "the full meal deal" and be a member of the 'clean plate gang'? (Loaded question)

NOTES

DAY 29: LISTEN

My sheep hear my voice, and I know them, and they follow me:

John 10:27

Dr. Doolittle is that lovable character that was portrayed first by Rex Harrison. Dr. Doolittle's greatest attribute was that he could not only talk to animals, but hear them as well. Not only did the animals love him, but it made him a very wealthy man.

Please do not send the orderlies in white coats to fetch me, but I also talked to my animals. Jesus said that His sheep know His voice; therefore, I believe my animals can be sensitized to recognize mine. And after all, I have heard some of you address your animals as well.

When you have stepped on the dog's paw or the cat's tail, and have apologized to them. "I'm so sorry Fluffy, they were all out of your favorite chicken chunks and gravy cat food." Have you ever told your child's hamster to stop turning that annoying wheel? "Polly wants a cracker?" "Where have you been Bongo I've been driving all over the neighborhood looking for you?"

It truly has been successful up to a point when I clap my hands and whistle for the sheep; they come when I call for "sheepies" but only when they are hungry of course. If I address them in a loud voice to not do something (such as not entering an open barn door), they respond as though I am speaking in Russian to a group of Canadians. They hear the words plainly and clearly, but don't have a clue what I am trying to communicate. I have somewhat better results with the cows, because when I clap my hands and yell, it usually means they get to move to a greener paddock of grass, or a treat of some sweet feed. The goats, as well as the cats equal each other in total disregard for anything I say.

I hear that some of us in the church have become like my farm animals. We only listen for the Great Shepherd's voice when it involves something selfish. We listen so intently when we need something from our Father, but turn a deaf ear when He asks us to do something that is unpleasant or out of our comfort zone, or cost us something.

It has been my experience that the Holy Spirit never yells; He only speaks in a still, small voice. For those of us who are hearing impaired, there are battery operated electronic devices which enable us to hear better. My wish is that there was a device that we could issue to our spirit to better hear the voice of the Lord. But wishes don't make it true.

The only way to hear His voice is, you guessed it,

LISTEN! So let's stop what we are doing, turn off and tune out all the ambient noise around you, and listen for the voice of the God of the universe. He is trying to get a hold... of you.

QUESTIONS

1. Would you rather listen or talk?

2. Do you hear the voice of the Lord more clearly through which of the following:

    a) Reading the Word.

    b) Listening i.e. Preaching, recorded messages or song.

    c) Prayer time.

    d) Life incidents.

3. Have you ever met someone who absolutely dominated the conversation you were in to the point you had no opportunity to answer a question or interject a comment?

4. When you talk to God (prayer) do you allow time for Him to answer?

NOTES

DAY 30: BIG DOG

Love not the world, neither the things that are in the world. If any man love the world, the love of the Father is not in him.

1 John 2:15

"Here's the plan," said Lambie to Midnight her sister. "You jump up and hit the dog food bucket and while farmer Dave is trying to save the dog food, I'll run out of the gate with Nanook the big dog. We will have so much fun romping through the pasture, because Nanook kind of likes me and watches over me."

"All right", said Midnight, "but make it fast".

Farmer Dave lunged forward, trying to save as much dog food as he could from hitting the ground. As he did, he left a big unprotected hole through the unlatched gate. Lambie leaped forward just like a deer, she had all four legs in the air as she bolted through the gate right behind Nanook, the Great Pyrenees dog. She could barely hear the farmers voice as he exclaimed, "Oh no, not again" because she was already well into the cow pasture, trying to keep up with Nanook.

The dog was very quick for her huge size and could easily run over the tall weeds on her way to the bottom where he knew the cool stream awaited. Lambie was now beginning to struggle somewhat running through the tall grass. This is so much fun she thought, I imagine every sheep and goat in the barn are so jealous of me. Just then Lambie realized Nanook's fluffy tail seemed a little farther ahead of her than she would have liked, after all he was her protector, or was he?

The small sheep stepped up the pace to catch up, but she was breathing very hard. Nanook reached the bottom with care, and bent his massive head into the cool creek, and began to lap up the clear water. Lambie was panting fast and furious when she got to the stream next to the dog. She too began to put her mouth into the stream, but since it was moving water, it went right up her nostril.

She drew back and snorted the water from her nostrils, which scared her because she couldn't breathe. Just then Nanook took off up the bank and began to run again through the lower pasture. Lambie, snorting and wheezing and sneezing took out after that guiding tail, still thirsty and much more tired than ever because she was only used to short sprints in the barn, pasture Nanook was racing up the hill to her friend Rusty's house, unaware and unconcerned that Lambie was way behind.

When the big dog crested the rise at the neighbor's

yard, he did not see Rusty or his chain leash outside, so Nanook headed toward home. Lambie was halfway up the hill when she got a glimpse of the big dog in yet another direction, still running. Lambie turned in a direction of the dog, but her pace was not even half of Nanook's speed. Doesn't he ever stop running, she thought, panting as she strained her muscles to lope through the very tall grass.

Nanook was nowhere in sight. Lambie was now filled with fear where excitement once danced in her small brain. She could only walk now, her muscles burning from overuse, her tongue hanging out of the side of her mouth, and scenes filling her heart at her foolish plan to leave the safety and comfort of the barn pasture. Her fear was now turned to hope as she crested the hill where she at last saw Nanook and spied the familiar red barn she knew so well. She was going home.

When Lambie finally got to the fence, her heart sunk because she realized she was on the wrong side and could not get through the fence. She had no clue where that awful dog Nanook had gone, and didn't care, she just wanted in. Lambie finally found a hole in the cattle fence which led her to a small patch of short grass and a brick house.

At that moment the farmer Dave's wife Shirley came down the steps from the house making some kind of utterance Lambie did not understand, but then she didn't speak human. She did recognize the tone of voice as being kind, concerned and soothing.

When Shirley reached Lambie she was shaking all over, even her long tail was bouncing from the muscle spasms. Lambie was home to the place she had been well cared for. There was Nanook lying under a shade tree, oblivious to the condition of the small sheep. Lambie was still shaking, but enjoying the gentle strokes and soothing words of her caretaker.

She longed to be back with her family and friends, but right now needed this comfort more. She would have a story to tell, but not the one she had written in her imagination. She had learned a lesson from today and probably would not go on another foolish adventure... Or would she?

How many times do we try to "run with the big dog" only to find we have made a mistake. We cannot love the things that the world does, because we are no longer of this world, our citizenship is in Heaven.

We pass through gates just because they are open. We climb over fences that are there for our protection. We follow after worldly big dogs instead of listening to the guiding, carrying voice of the Good Shepherd, Jesus. Let us take time to follow our master instead of rashly changing course off of the straight and narrow pathway, just to satisfy a whim or a promising worldly venture. Our spiritual well-being depends on that.

QUESTIONS

1. Have you ever been a member of a gang, club, or other organization where you felt you just didn't fit?

2. In your own life, what 'big dog' should you stay away from?

3. Have you ever seen a Christian out mingling with the wrong crowd of people? What did you do?

4. In golf a novice player is encouraged to always play alongside someone who is better than they are. Do you think it is OK for us as Christians to associate with others who can help us to do better and get ahead?

NOTES

DAY 31: TINY EARTHWORM

What is man, that thou shouldest magnify him? and that thou shouldest set thine heart upon him?

Job 7:17

Much like a teenage boy, a chicken would eat about anything you set before him. I was cleaning out the barn one day, and as I moved a storage skid so I could sweep under it, a nest of small mice presented itself. Before you can say "get the mouse trap" my chickens were tearing apart the mouse house with the ferocity of a hungry lioness on a fresh kill. The tiny rodents were gone in less time than it would take to quote the above verse. I was amazed, saddened, and grateful in that order.

Brother Job knew all too well the insignificance and the fragility of man as he had just experienced the loss of all of his children who were all killed in a tragedy prepared by Satan, our adversary.

I was digging up our flower bed in preparation to do some planting. As I was crushing a clump of dirt in my hand, I noticed a portion of the clump had something wiggling out of it. It was about one inch long and had the thickness of a strand of angel hair spaghetti. It was trying to bury itself deeper into the earth, to hide itself from the giant hand that had unearthed it.

Carefully letting everything in my open hand fall to the ground, the small earthworm was nakedly revealed in my outstretched hand. After it's identification I considered tossing it aimlessly toward a nearby chicken knowing of course it would become an instant food source for the birds. But the more I studied this small creature, the more I realized he was not all that different in his relationship to me, as my life was to a great God.

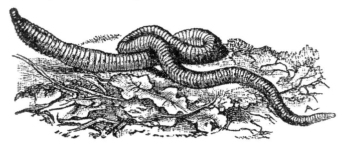

How often did I believe I was playing a brilliant overture with my life, only to have God bring me to the realization I had only been banging out chopsticks? (After all) Compared to His masterpiece, I couldn't even create a tiny earthworm, let alone planet Earth as He had done.

King David said, "What is man that thou art mindful of him?" The only explanation for that question is to be found in John 3:16: "For God so loved the world that He gave His only begotten Son."

Man was the last creation in the book of Genesis, and we were made in His image. I suppose He was pleased with His artistic fashioning of man in his own image. I am so glad that we are fearfully and wonderfully made. We should take pride in that fact, not prideful of our accomplishments.

Bear in mind when you think you are really something, remember the tiny earthworm. After putting everything into perspective, I gently lowered the earthworm back to the ground from whence he came. And he melded into the freshly turned earth of the flower garden, ready to resume what he was created to do.

QUESTIONS

1. On a scale of 1 – 5 (5 being the largest) what number of importance would you assign to yourself in relation to other people?

2. Looking at yourself from God's perspective, what number would you rate yourself?

3. The tiny earthworm experienced what it was like to live at the mercy of a giant that was 10,000 times larger than himself. How do you think we should respond to God in which we are infinitesimally smaller?

NOTES

ABOUT THE AUTHOR

David William Treat was born in the city of Philadelphia, Pennsylvania, but he is just a down to earth character who had his head and heart lifted to heavenly places after encountering the living God.

His early adult years found him serving in the U.S. Navy as a Hospital Corpsman and he was attached to the Third Marines while serving in Viet Nam.

After experiencing an epiphany of Jesus in 1986 he entered the ministry and has served in that capacity for 28 years. Since his retirement, he and his wife Shirley moved to a working farm in Southern Tennessee, where he has now picked up a pen along with a pitchfork.